His Name Was Nicholas

Full Script & Score

By Eric & Lana Elder

His Name Was Nicholas:
Full Script & Score by Eric & Lana Elder

12/16/2021

Based on the book
St. Nicholas: The Believer
by Eric & Lana Elder.

Cover Art: *Nicholas in the Snow* by Bo Elder.

Lyrics for "Is There Room For Me?"
by Annette Carden-Dale.

Special thanks to Jo, Bo, and Kaleo Elder
for their invaluable help with the melodies, lyrics,
and chord progressions of these songs.

ISBN: 978-1-931760-78-2

Full Script
Including Lyrics

To listen to song samples
& orchestrations, visit:
HisNameWasNicholas.com

DEDICATION

To my sweet wife, Lana,
who inspired and helped me
tell this spectacular story.

You made the most of your dash.

12/25/1963 - 11/15/2012

ABOUT THE STORY

His Name Was Nicholas is based on the real-life story of a man named Nicholas who lived on the northern coast of the Mediterranean Sea in the 3rd and 4th centuries AD. His faith in Christ made such a difference in his life, and the lives of those he touched, that he was eventually dubbed "Saint Nicholas," the forerunner of our modern-day Santa Claus.

Many people, however, have never heard his real-life story, so this show will serve as a heartwarming introduction to this man who loved Jesus with all his heart, soul, mind, and strength.

Beyond the historical accuracy of the main elements in this show, we've also infused it with tenderhearted moments of love and laughter with brand new characters who help bring his story to life. A list of "What We Know" about Nicholas is included at the end of the script.

The tagline for the show says, "Nicholas had just one life to live, but if he lived it right, one life was all he would need." My hope is that this story will demonstrate, in a real and tangible way, the power of one person to touch the world for good.

May you be inspired to do the same and be blessed as you do!

Eric Elder

CAST

NICHOLAS - our hero, age 19-65 as he ages through the show
YOUNG NICK - our hero at age 9
NICK'S FATHER - our hero's father and inspiration
NICK'S MOTHER - our hero's mother and teacher
NICK'S UNCLE - our hero's uncle and caregiver
DIMITRI - our storyteller and Nicholas's guide, age 20-56
YOUNG DIMITRI - our storyteller at age 10-14
SAMMY - Nicholas's light-hearted guide at age 9-13
RUTHIE - Nicholas's sharp-as-a-tack guide at age 8-12
SHIP'S CAPTAIN - an experienced, faith-filled captain
YOUNG SHIPMATE - an inexperienced, fear-filled shipmate
THE HOLY SPIRIT - a graceful dancer who leads and comforts
THREE PRIESTS - a devout and charming trio
SOPHIA - a love-torn young woman, age 18
CECILIA - a love-seeking young woman, age 16
ANNA MARIA - a love-inspired young woman, age 18-54
YOUNG ANNA MARIA - our flower seller at age 12
CASSIUS - Sophia's heartthrob
MIGEL - the disheartened father of our three young women
CONSTANTINE - the first Christian emperor of Rome
ARIUS - an orator whose words end abruptly

PLUS VARIOUS TOWNSPEOPLE of Patara, Myra, Nicaea, and the Holy Land, including MEN, WOMEN, CHILDREN, CREW MATES, SOLDIERS, PRIESTS, BISHOPS, and a CHILDREN'S CHOIR.

SETTING

The story takes place on the coast of the Mediterranean where Nicholas lived and traveled during the 3rd and 4th centuries AD.

PROLOGUE - Patara (now known as Gelemiş, Turkey)
ACT 1 - Patara
ACT 2 - The Holy Land (now known as Israel and Palestine)
ACT 3 - The Great Sea (now known as the Mediterranean Sea)
ACT 4 - Myra (now known as Demre, Turkey)
ACT 5 - The Prison (a Roman prison somewhere in Asia)
ACT 6 - The Palace (at Nicaea, now known as Iznik, Turkey)
EPILOGUE - Patara

SCENES

SONGS

PROLOGUE - THE SAINT

DIMITRI sits on a high stool lit by a single spotlight, stage left. NICHOLAS lies on his bed, stage right, inside a small bedroom in his home. He is surrounded by a few people at his bedside including ANNA MARIA. Another spotlight highlights a wooden staff made of smooth driftwood propped against a wall near his bed. This staff will be highlighted throughout the story.

DIMITRI

My name is Dimitri... Dimitri Alexander. But that's not important. What's important is that man over there, lying on his bed. He's, well, I suppose there's really no better way to describe him except to say... he's a saint. Not simply because of all the good he's done, but because he was, as a saint always is, a *Believer*. He believed there was Someone in life who was greater than him, Someone who guided him, Someone who walked with him through every one of his days.

If you were to look at him closely, lying there on his bed, it might look to you as if he were asleep. And in some sense I guess you'd be right. But the truth is he's more awake now than he's ever been.

My friends and I have come here today to spend his last day on earth with him. A few minutes ago we watched as he passed from this life to the next.

I should be crying, I know. Believe me, I have been, and I will be again. But for now, I can't help but be grateful that he has finally made it to his new home, a home he has been dreaming about for many years. A home where he can finally talk to God face to face, like I'm talking to you right now.

Oh, he was a saint all right. But to me and to so many others, he was something even more. He was... how could I put it? An inspiration. A friend. A teacher. A helper. A giver. Oh, he loved to give and give and give some more, until it seemed he had nothing left to give at all. But then he'd reach down deep and find a little more. "There's always something you can give," he used to say.

He always hoped, in some small way, that he could use his life to make a difference in the world. He wanted, above all, to help people. But with so many needs all around, what could he possibly do?

He was like a man on a beach surrounded by starfish, thousands of which had been washed up on shore. He knew they would die if they didn't make it back into the water.

Not knowing how to save them all, he did what he could. He reached down, picked one up, and tossed it back into the water. Then he reached down again, picked up another, and did the same.

When someone asked him why he bothered, how he could possibly make a difference with so many that needed help, he just picked up another starfish and tossed it into the water. "It made a difference to that one," he said. Then he reached down and picked up another.

You see, to the world you may be just one person, but to one person you may be the world.

In many ways, my friend was just like you and me. Each of us has one life to live. But if you live it right, one life is all you need. And if you live your life for God, well, you just might touch the whole world.

Did his life make any difference? I already know my answer because I'm one of those he reached down and picked up many, many years ago. But how about I tell you his story, and when I get to the end I'll let you decide if his life made a difference or not. Then maybe, by the time we're finished, you'll see that *your* life can make a difference, too.

Oh, by the way, I haven't told you his name yet, this man who was such a great saint, such a great believer in the God who loved him, created him, and with whom he is now living forever.

His name was Nicholas... and *this* is his story.

1. ST. NICK'S THEME

The opening song kicks off at full tilt with a flurry of activity erupting on stage. Women carry packages, men carry Christmas trees, a horse pulls a sleigh, children slide on sleds, all criss-crossing the stage from various angles. Images of Christmas appear all around the stage, both physically and projected onto screens, including ornaments, bells, cookies, gingerbread houses, reindeer, Santa Claus, snowflakes, and a single, radiant star over Bethlehem.

When the song ends, the lights FADE TO BLACK.

ACT 1, SCENE 1 - THE HUNT

As the lights come up, we see the same room in the same home, stage right, but NICHOLAS and his visitors are gone and YOUNG NICK and NICK'S FATHER have appeared. The wooden staff still stands in the same spot against the wall, but otherwise the home is decorated with a few newer, fresher items of a young family. YOUNG NICK and NICK'S FATHER are preparing to go on a walk through the city.

YOUNG NICK
(excitedly)
Who's it going to be today, father?

NICK'S FATHER
We won't know till God shows us, Nicholas.

YOUNG NICK
(curiously)
But how will we know?

NICK'S FATHER
Oh, we'll know. Keep your eyes open wide, and He'll show us.

YOUNG NICK
Like a treasure hunt!

NICK'S FATHER
Yes, like a treasure hunt! Today, it's oranges. Three oranges for three people God will show us. You can't let them see you, though, Nicholas. That's part of the fun. God uses us to be His hands, but we want all the glory to go to Him. Are you ready?

YOUNG NICK
Ready?!? Who *wouldn't* want to go on a treasure hunt?

YOUNG NICK opens the door as NICK'S FATHER picks up his wooden staff from against the wall. They exit the home and start walking across the stage. The house slides off stage right as YOUNG NICK and NICK'S FATHER step onto a conveyor belt traversing the stage, walking in place as the belt travels beneath them. YOUNG NICK looks at his father and begins to sing.

2. WHO'S IT GOING TO BE TODAY?

YOUNG NICK

WHO'S IT GOING TO BE TODAY, FATHER?
WHO'S IT GOING TO BE TODAY?
WHO'S IT GOING TO BE TODAY, FATHER?
WHO'S IT GOING TO BE TODAY?

NICK'S FATHER

WE WON'T KNOW TILL WE KNOW,
BUT WE'LL KNOW WHEN HE SHOWS US.
EVEN THOUGH WE DON'T KNOW,
WE WILL GO, AND HE'LL SHOW US.

YOUNG NICK

WHO'S IT GOING TO BE TODAY, FATHER?
WHO'S IT GOING TO BE TODAY?
WHO'S IT GOING TO BE TODAY, FATHER?
WHO'S IT GOING TO BE TODAY?

NICK'S FATHER

EVEN THOUGH WE DON'T KNOW,
WE WILL KNOW WHEN HE SHOWS US.
SO WE'LL GO, THEN WE'LL KNOW,
YES, WE'LL KNOW WHEN HE SHOWS US.

(YOUNG NICK gives his father a puzzled look)

NICK'S FATHER (CONT'D)

EVEN THOUGH WE DON'T KNOW,

(spoken)

YOU WILL KNOW, YES, YOU'LL KNOW.

YOUNG NICK

EVEN THOUGH WE DON'T KNOW,
WE WILL KNOW?

TOGETHER

(YOUNG NICK looks up at his father who looks up to *his* Father in heaven)

WHO'S IT GOING TO BE TODAY, FATHER?
WHO'S IT GOING TO BE TODAY?
WHO'S IT GOING TO BE TODAY, FATHER?
WHO'S IT GOING TO BE TODAY?

(looking at each other)
WE WON'T KNOW TILL WE KNOW,
BUT WE'LL KNOW WHEN HE SHOWS US.
EVEN THOUGH WE DON'T KNOW,
WE WILL GO, AND HE'LL SHOW US.
(looking out to see if they see anyone)
SO WE'LL GO, THEN WE'LL KNOW,
YES, WE'LL KNOW WHEN HE SHOWS US!
EVEN THOUGH WE DON'T KNOW,
WE WILL GO!!!

YOUNG NICK
WHO WILL IT BE?
TELL ME WHO WILL WE SEE?

NICK'S FATHER
KEEP YOUR EYES OPEN WIDE, AND YOU WILL SEE...

The music trails off as the eyes of both YOUNG NICK and NICK'S FATHER land on the same child, lying on the ground with his head on his mother's lap, both sleeping. They have appeared via a conveyor belt pulling them slowly into view.

YOUNG NICK and NICK'S FATHER look at each other with knowing looks. YOUNG NICK reaches into his pocket and looks at his father to see what he thinks. NICK'S FATHER nods in agreement, and YOUNG NICK walks inconspicuously toward the sleeping mother and son, putting an orange under the mother's wrap which lays over them both.

YOUNG NICK sneaks back to his father and they smile at each other, both of them pulling out from their pockets their remaining oranges. The music starts again, and they finish their song together.

TOGETHER
WHO'S IT GOING TO BE TODAY, FATHER?
WHO'S IT GOING TO BE TODAY?
WHO'S IT GOING TO BE TODAY, FATHER?
WHO'S IT GOING TO BE TODAY?
WHO'S IT GOING TO BE TODAY?
WHO'S IT GOING TO BE TODAY?

They exit stage left as the lights FADE TO BLACK.

ACT 1, SCENE 2 - THE HEALING

As the lights come up, YOUNG NICK'S home glides back into place on stage right where NICK'S MOTHER is getting things ready for dinner. YOUNG NICK and NICK'S FATHER cross the stage from stage left and re-enter the home, excitedly. As they put away their cloaks and the wooden staff, they eagerly tell NICK'S MOTHER all that happened.

YOUNG NICK
You should have seen them, Mother! When that boy woke up, he looked at that orange as if it was made of gold!

NICK'S FATHER
Then we found a girl on a hill picking flowers and putting them in her basket. Nicholas snuck up and added an orange to her basket, too. She turned her head in every direction trying to see who put the orange in her basket!

YOUNG NICK
And when Father saw Grandma Dumpling making breakfast in her kitchen, he crouched down and set the last orange on her window sill where she would surely see it when she sat down to eat!

NICK'S MOTHER
You two and your treasure hunts! Anyone else would think you had discovered ~~a chest of~~ gold.

NICK'S FATHER
And we have, my dear. Gold, locked away in people's hearts, waiting to be discovered. And your heart is the most golden of all.

He pulls out some flowers wrapped in a cloth.

NICK'S FATHER (CONT'D)
I found them on the hill where we saw the girl with her basket.

He gives his wife a kiss on the cheek.

NICK'S MOTHER
You're the best! Both of you. You're always thinking of others. Don't you ever think of yourselves?

NICK'S FATHER
Of course we do! God loves us, too. But He blesses us to be a blessing. As Jesus said, "Freely you have received, freely give." And if you look around, there's always something you can give.

YOUNG NICK
Can you tell me more stories about Jesus tonight, Father?

NICK'S FATHER
Yes, but first get ready for dinner, Nicholas. Your mother's been working hard for us. Then we'll tell some stories. Tonight! About healing!

YOUNG NICK
Yes, sir!

YOUNG NICK rushes out of the room and offstage.

NICK'S MOTHER
(quietly)
I'm glad you took him with you today. I've been so worried, though. Did you learn any more about the cobbler's son?

NICK'S FATHER
(both taking a seat)
His symptoms are exactly the same as those who died in Myra. Half their city has already succumbed to it.

NICK'S MOTHER
So it's true, then. The plague has arrived here, too. What can we do?

NICK'S FATHER
The same thing we always do, my love. Ask God what to do, then do what He says and trust Him completely. Only now the stakes are higher than ever before. But fear and panic will never help us. Only faith. Faith... and hope... and love.

YOUNG NICK returns and takes his place at the table.

YOUNG NICK
Have you ever seen the writings yourself, Father, the stories of Jesus written on the parchments?

NICK'S FATHER
Only once, Nicholas, but once is enough to change someone for life. Even though it's been almost two hundred years since Luke and Paul came through here in Patara, they shared the stories with our whole city.

They said the stories had been written down by some of Jesus' followers. Luke wrote down many of the stories, too, after asking those who had seen what had happened with their own eyes.

YOUNG NICK
I want to go there one day, Father, to the land where Jesus walked. Do you think I can go some day?

NICK'S FATHER
Some day, yes. It's only a few weeks by boat around the sea, of course. But it's not an easy voyage. Maybe when you're older you can venture out and see it for yourself.

The table is ready, and NICK'S FATHER indicates it's time to pray.

NICK'S FATHER (CONT'D)
Father, thank You for these gifts that have come from Your hand. We bless Your name. Please bless the hands that have prepared it and us to Your service. In Jesus' name, Amen.

YOUNG NICK
(all begin to eat)
What kind of healings did He do, Father, this Jesus?

NICK'S FATHER
Oh, one time He made a paste of mud and put it on a blind man's eyes. When the man washed it off, he could see! Another time, a soldier came to Jesus saying his faithful servant was sick.

When Jesus saw the soldier’s faith, He spoke a word and the man’s servant was healed that very moment, even though he was very far away.

It was different every time, Nicholas. Why, one time, He asked two blind men if they believed He could heal them. They said, “Yes,” and He said, “According to your faith will it be done.” ~~Suddenly, they could see!~~

YOUNG NICK

How did He do it? How did He heal so many people?

NICK'S MOTHER

(after looking at NICK'S FATHER and remembering their previous conversation)

I suppose He did it by asking His Father in heaven to send a bit of heaven here to earth. All healing comes from heaven, you know.

YOUNG NICK

(thinking)

But what about the time *you* healed me, Mother, when I cut my hand, and you wrapped it up?

NICK'S MOTHER

(laughing)

All I did was wash it off, give it a kiss, and put a bandage on it... long enough for your body to do the healing work God designed it to do. Yes, I helped patch it together, but even that healing came from heaven.

Or when your father broke his leg, the doctor put a splint on it to hold it straight, but it was God who did the healing, knitting his bones back together. We simply did the waiting.

As I see it, *all* healing comes from heaven, for in heaven there’s no pain, no sickness, no death. And when Jesus healed people, I imagine He must have asked His Father to send a bit of heaven here to earth, the same way He taught His disciples to pray, saying, “Your kingdom come, Your will be done, on earth as it is in heaven.”

Yes, healing comes from heaven, of that you can be sure...

NICK'S MOTHER begins to sing.

3. HEALING COMES FROM HEAVEN

NICK'S MOTHER

HEALING COMES FROM HEAVEN,
OF THAT YOU CAN BE SURE,
WHETHER BLOOD THAT SLOWS WHILE BLEEDING
OR THE BONES THAT MEND AND GROW.

YES, HEALING COMES FROM HEAVEN,
OF THAT YOU CAN BE SURE.
WE HAVE JUST TO REACH TOWARD HEAVEN
AND THEN WATCH THE HEALING FLOW!

(she holds YOUNG NICK'S hand)
SOMETIMES IT COMES SO QUICK,
WE HARDLY UNDERSTAND.
(she points to NICK'S FATHER'S leg)
SOMETIMES IT TAKES SO LONG,
BUT THEN WE STAND!
AND WE CAN ALWAYS KNOW
THAT ONE DAY WE WILL
BE MADE WHOLE
WHEN HEAVEN COMES TO STAY.

NICK'S FATHER

HEALING COMES FROM HEAVEN,
OF THAT YOU CAN BE SURE.
EVEN FATHERS, MOTHERS, DOCTORS
KNOW THAT GOD'S THE ONE WHO CURES.

YES, HEALING COMES FROM HEAVEN,
OF THAT YOU CAN BE SURE,
SO WE PRAY TO GOD IN HEAVEN NOW
TO TOUCH US HERE ON EARTH!

YOUNG NICK

(looking at his fingers)
SOMETIMES IT COMES SO QUICK,
WE HARDLY UNDERSTAND.

NICK'S FATHER

SOMETIMES IT TAKES SO LONG,
BUT THEN WE STAND.

ALL TOGETHER
AND WE CAN ALWAYS KNOW
THAT ONE DAY WE WILL
BE MADE WHOLE
WHEN HEAVEN COMES TO STAY.

YOUNG NICK
HEALING COMES FROM HEAVEN...

NICK'S FATHER
YES, HEALING COMES FROM HEAVEN...

NICK'S MOTHER
(looking up to heaven, as a prayer)
PLEASE SEND A BIT OF HEAVEN OUR WAY.

FADE TO BLACK.

ACT 1, SCENE 3 - THE LIFE

When the lights come up, it's the next morning with the sun streaming in the window. NICK'S FATHER, NICK'S MOTHER, and YOUNG NICK are in the kitchen preparing for the day.

YOUNG NICK

(excitedly)

Who's it going to be today, Father?

NICK'S FATHER

(somber, but not depressed)

We have a different kind of blessing we're going to give today, Nicholas. Our hands... our hearts... our ears.

YOUNG NICK

(puzzled)

How can you give away your hands or your heart or you *ears*?

NICK'S FATHER

(laughing)

You don't give them away, really. You just lend them out for a bit. You use your hands to help in whatever way someone might need it.. cooking, cleaning, washing. You use your heart to show you care. And you use your ears to listen... to listen to whatever they might need to say, to help them let out some of the fire that might be burning them up from the inside. You lend them your hands, your heart, your ears... you see?

YOUNG NICK

I see.

He then realizes they must know already who needs their help.

YOUNG NICK (CONT'D)

What's wrong? Who needs our help? What do they need?

NICK'S MOTHER
(taking a cue from the nod of NICK'S FATHER)
It's the cobbler's son. He's very sick, and we're going to visit them to see what we can do.

YOUNG NICK
If he's very sick, Mother, maybe we shouldn't go? Maybe we would get sick, too?

NICK'S MOTHER
(nodding in agreement)
That's very wise, Nicholas. Sometimes people need time to heal on their own and so the sickness doesn't spread. But other times, they need our help. This is one of those times. We've prayed, we've asked God what He wants us to do, and this is what He's put on our hearts. It's not always easy, Nicholas, doing what God wants us to do. Giving doesn't always mean giving your oranges or your silver or even your gold. Sometimes giving is much more costly than any of those things.

YOUNG NICK
More costly than gold?

NICK'S MOTHER
Giving your time... your hands, your heart, your ears... any of those can certainly be more costly than gold! But there's one thing we can't do, Nicholas. We can't outgive God. He's already given us more than we could ever repay. So if there's something He wants us to do, and we can possibly do it, we need to try.

YOUNG NICK
But what if *you* get sick, Mother?

NICK'S MOTHER
We hope and pray we don't, Nicholas. But we can trust if God has called us to do something, He will help us to do it. In some ways, it's so simple. But in other ways, it's the hardest thing to do... doing whatever God asks (she looks at NICK'S FATHER).

NICK'S FATHER

It's always good to count the cost, Nicholas. But in the end, your Mother's absolutely right. We can never outgive God. Some fears are good, Nicholas. They keep us alive. But some fears keep us from living... truly living. Don't ever let the fear of dying keep you from living the life God wants you to live. Everyone dies eventually, Nicholas, but not everyone truly lives.

NICK'S FATHER reaches out to take hold of his staff, which is leaning against the wall.

YOUNG NICK

Why do you still have that old staff, Father? Why don't you get a new one. I've seen some brightly polished ones down by the pier, just unloaded from ships.

NICK'S FATHER

Oh, I don't mind this one, Nicholas. In fact, I like it very much. You know I found it on the beach one day, a piece of driftwood, sanded smooth by the wind and the waves. It was the perfect length to help me climb the hill as I walked, and it was just the right size to ward off a few unexpected "visitors" that I encountered in the brush beside the path. No, you don't need to be an old man to need something, or Someone, to lean on once in a while, just a wise one.

NICK'S MOTHER

And your father's the wisest man I've ever met. Which is, of course, one of the reasons I married him.

She looks lovingly, yet honestly a bit anxiously, at NICK'S FATHER.

NICK'S FATHER

Time to go now. There's work to do that our Father wants done today.

They exit the house as the lights FADE TO BLACK.

ACT 1, SCENE 4 - THE COBBLER

YOUNG NICK, NICK'S FATHER, and NICK'S MOTHER are walking up to THE COBBLER'S house when a TOWNSPERSON joins them.

TOWNSPERSON
You're not going in there are you? Aren't you afraid of the plague?

NICK'S FATHER
Yes, we're going in, and yes, we're very afraid of the plague. But we can't leave them on their own at a time like this. Now is when they need us most.

TOWNSPERSON
What do they need? What can we possibly do?

YOUNG NICK
We won't know till we get there, isn't that what you said, Father? God will show us when we get there. Right?

NICK'S FATHER
That's right, Nicholas. But we're not going empty-handed. We've brought some food and supplies to keep them going for a few days so they can attend to their son. Most of all, we hope to encourage them that God hasn't left them alone.

NICK'S MOTHER
Sometimes what people need most is to know that someone cares. If we can do that, it will be worth it.

TOWNSPERSON
(fearfully)
I've heard the cobblers aren't the only ones who've been infected. It's already spreading to others... the mayor, the baker, and the vine keeper on the hill near here.

NICK'S MOTHER
(fearlessly)
If you hear of more, let us know. We can only help if we know who needs us.

The TOWNSPERSON walks on and NICK'S FATHER knocks on the door. After a deliberate pause, THE COBBLER opens the door, hesitantly.

THE COBBLER
Yes?

NICK'S FATHER
We've heard about your son. We've come to help.

THE COBBLER
Bless you. We could use it. Come in, come in.

YOUNG NICK'S family enters the house where the mother is cradling her youthful son in her arms. The son is coughing sporadically, a visible sign of this particular plague.

NICK'S MOTHER
What can we do to help?

THE COBBLER'S WIFE
We could use some food. We haven't been able to go out, fearful of what others might think, but more fearful we might spread the plague. Our son needs strength, though. If you could get us something to eat and say a prayer for us, that would be an answer to ours.

NICK'S MOTHER
We've brought some food with us, and the prayers are already on their way to heaven. Let me help you get something ready.

While NICK'S MOTHER unpacks and prepares some food for the family, YOUNG NICK, NICK'S FATHER, and THE COBBLER go near the window. YOUNG NICK looks outside.

THE COBBLER
(to NICK'S FATHER)
Thank you. Not many people would have the faith to do what you've just done.

YOUNG NICK
Look, Father, you can see the snow on the mountain peak from here!

THE COBBLER
It seems its always covered in snow this time of year. It's a beautiful sight every time I see

it. Of course, it hardly ever snows down here on the coast.

YOUNG NICK
Hardly ever? You mean it's snowed before here in Patara?!?

THE COBBLER
Yes, but hardly ever. It only happens maybe once every twenty years. I've only seen it snow down here twice in my whole life.

YOUNG NICK
I hope I can see it sometime!

THE COBBLER
You might, son, you just might. But if you ever see it snow here on the coast, that would be a special day, indeed.

NICK'S FATHER
I've only seen it once in my lifetime, Nicholas...

As they're conversing, a TOWNSPERSON knocks hard on the door, then bursts in.

TOWNSPERSON
(stammering to get it out)
It's the baker... The baker... He's dead!

The announcement sends a shock wave through everyone in the house. The TOWNSPERSON leaves, moving on to alert the next household. Their shock is palpable because they know from nearby cities that while this may have been the first such announcement, it won't be the last. In fact, it's just the beginning.

FADE TO BLACK.

ACT 1, SCENE 5 - THE PLAGUE

As the plague continues to ravage the town, everyone wonders who will be next to succumb to its deadly effects. YOUNG NICK, NICK'S FATHER, and NICK'S MOTHER are once again at home, having returned from going throughout the city to see who they could help in their most desperate time of need.

NICK'S MOTHER

(concerned)

That makes twenty-three. When will it stop? What else can we do?

NICK'S FATHER

We can only trust that God is answering our prayers... in His way... in His time.

YOUNG NICK enters the room, having stood visibly behind the doorway and having heard the grim statistic. He asks his father once again "Who's It Going To Be Today?" but this time sung in a minor key, reprising the earlier version of the same song as when they were looking for people to bless with oranges.

4. WHO'S IT GOING TO BE TODAY? (MINOR)

YOUNG NICK

WHO'S IT GOING TO BE TODAY, FATHER?
WHO'S IT GOING TO BE TODAY?
WHO'S IT GOING TO BE TODAY, FATHER?
WHO'S IT GOING TO BE TODAY?

NICK'S FATHER

WE WON'T KNOW TILL WE KNOW,
BUT WE'LL KNOW WHEN HE SHOWS US.
EVEN THOUGH WE DON'T KNOW,
WE WILL GO, AND HE'LL SHOW US.

NICK'S MOTHER

(drying dishes and looking to heaven)

WHO'S IT GOING TO BE TODAY, FATHER?
WHO'S IT GOING TO BE TODAY?
WHO'S IT GOING TO BE TODAY, FATHER?
WHO'S IT GOING TO BE TODAY?

NICK'S FATHER

(in response to the prayer of NICK'S MOTHER)

EVEN THOUGH WE DON'T KNOW,
WE WILL KNOW WHEN HE SHOWS US.
SO WE'LL GO, THEN WE'LL KNOW,
YES, WE'LL KNOW WHEN HE SHOWS US.

EVEN THOUGH WE DON'T KNOW,
(spoken)
WE WILL KNOW,
YES, WE'LL KNOW.

YOUNG NICK

(spoken)
WE WILL KNOW...?

YOUNG NICK, NICK'S MOTHER, and NICK'S FATHER all walk out to the street as the townspeople begin to sing.

ALL TOWNSPEOPLE

(looking to each other and to heaven)
WHO'S IT GOING TO BE TODAY, FATHER?
WHO'S IT GOING TO BE TODAY?
WHO'S IT GOING TO BE TODAY, FATHER?
WHO'S IT GOING TO BE TODAY?

WE WON'T KNOW TILL WE KNOW,
BUT WE'LL KNOW WHEN HE SHOWS US.
EVEN THOUGH WE DON'T KNOW,
WE WILL GO, AND HE'LL SHOW US.
(all look left, then right)
SO WE'LL GO, THEN WE'LL KNOW,
YES, WE'LL KNOW WHEN HE SHOWS US.
WE WILL GO.

YOUNG NICK

WHO WILL IT BE?
TELL ME WHO WILL WE SEE?

NICK'S FATHER

KEEP YOUR EYES OPEN WIDE, AND YOU WILL SEE...

A spotlight comes up on NICK'S MOTHER, who has found a young boy and his siblings in the street. All are crying while NICK'S MOTHER sits on the ground and cradles the boy in her arms. She begins singing the most beautiful lullaby for him, a reprise of "Healing Comes From

Heaven" in the original, major key. She rocks him and gently strokes his face.

NICK'S MOTHER

HEALING COMES FROM HEAVEN,
OF THAT YOU CAN BE SURE,
WHETHER BLOOD THAT SLOWS WHILE BLEEDING
OR THE BONES THAT MEND AND GROW.

YES, HEALING COMES FROM HEAVEN,
OF THAT YOU CAN BE SURE.
WE HAVE JUST TO REACH TOWARD HEAVEN
AND THEN WATCH THE HEALING FLOW!

SOMETIMES IT COMES SO QUICK,
WE HARDLY UNDERSTAND.
SOMETIMES IT TAKES SO LONG,
BUT THEN WE STAND!

AND WE CAN ALWAYS KNOW
THAT ONE DAY WE WILL
BE MADE WHOLE
WHEN HEAVEN COMES TO STAY.

She closes the boy's eyes, and everyone knows he has just passed from this life to the next. The TOWNSPEOPLE have been watching this touching scene, but then come back to the question on everyone's mind. They look away and around and toward each other again, walking to the front of the stage as they sing.

ALL TOWNSPEOPLE

WHO'S IT GOING TO BE TODAY, FATHER?
WHO'S IT GOING TO BE TODAY?
WHO'S IT GOING TO BE TODAY, FATHER?
WHO'S IT GOING TO BE TODAY?

WHO'S IT GOING TO BE TODAY?
WHO'S IT GOING TO BE TODAY?
WHO'S IT GOING TO BE TODAY?

They strike their final pose, facing the audience, and the lights FADE TO BLACK.

ACT 1, SCENE 6 - THE SEA

NICK'S FATHER stands by the sea, leaning on his staff and contemplating the future as he looks out over the waves. After a moment, NICK'S MOTHER joins him.

NICK'S MOTHER

I knew I'd find you here. You always love the sea when you need to think.

NICK'S FATHER

It helps me clear my mind. Looking out over the sea is like looking out over eternity. I always make my best decisions here... in light of eternity.

My father used to go to the graveyard to make his decisions. He'd look at the stones that marked the spots where people were buried. Oftentimes, there was just a name, a date of birth, and a date of death, with a dash in between. He would look at that dash and say, "We know so little about them. Only when they were born and when they died. But what they did with their lives was up to them. How they used their time, the decisions they made, their secrets, their regrets. Those were all buried with them."

I want to live my life with no regrets. I want to live my life in a way that makes a difference.

NICK'S MOTHER

(coughing now)

It's not just hypothetical anymore, is it? Eternity, I mean. This is where our faith really comes in, doesn't it? Either we believe all we've believed up till now or we give it all up. But we can't give it up, can we? Where else would we turn if not to God who's brought us through so much already?

NICK'S FATHER

There's no where else! He's the One we've trusted up to this point. And He'll walk us through this next step, too.

He coughs, and we know he has the sickness as well. They hug and hold each other closely, looking out over eternity.

NICK'S MOTHER

What's going to happen to Nicholas? It looks like the sickness hasn't touched him yet.

NICK'S FATHER

And I pray it never will. God, I pray it never will. He's strong in his faith. I have to trust the same God who takes care of us will take care of him. I know God will give him the strength to get through anything.

Unaware that YOUNG NICK has discovered them on the beach and is walking up behind them, they're startled to hear him speak.

YOUNG NICK

Strength to get through what, Father? What will God need to give me strength for?

NICK'S MOTHER tries to hold back her tears, but instead begins coughing and takes a step backwards. YOUNG NICK knows. He stands paralyzed in the moment. NICK'S MOTHER wants to step back further, but doesn't. She, too, stands paralyzed in the moment.

Suddenly, YOUNG NICK breaks the stalemate. He runs to his mother. They hug, rocking and holding each other close. NICK'S FATHER puts his arms around them both. All three hold on to each other until the time is ripe for someone to speak. NICK'S FATHER fills the space with his rich words.

NICK'S FATHER

Some people think we've been foolish to do what we've been doing. But you know the truth, Nicholas. No one is a fool to give up a life he can't keep to gain a life he can't lose.

Even if it costs us everything we have, we've gained more than we could ever give. You can't outgive God, Nicholas. Everything we've done, we've done out of love. And as Jesus said, "Greater love has no one than this, that he lay down his life for his friends."

You're not just our son, Nicholas, you're our friend, too. Always remember how very much God loves you and how very much we love you. Promise me you'll remember this, Nicholas. Please, promise me.

YOUNG NICK looks from his father to his mother, then back again to his father, nodding in agreement. He knows he can trust his father, who trusts so fully in *his* Father.

FADE TO BLACK.

ACT 1, SCENE 7 - THE STAFF

YOUNG NICK sits on a chair by his father's empty bed. The staff stands in its usual spot against the wall. YOUNG NICK is waiting, with his head down, but for what, we don't know.

NICK'S UNCLE knocks at the door and steps in. He's dressed in monk's clothing... simple, but recognizable as a man of the cloth. He's kind, genuine, and full of grace.

NICK'S UNCLE
Ready, Nicholas? Have everything you need?

YOUNG NICK
Almost ready, Uncle.

YOUNG NICK picks up a bag he's packed and crosses the room to his uncle. They embrace. YOUNG NICK looks around, wishing he could stay in this room forever. NICK'S UNCLE sees how torn he is.

NICK'S UNCLE
I know you'll miss it here, Nicholas, but your father was convinced you should come live with us at the monastery. I know you're big enough to take care of yourself, and I know you don't want to leave here. But I trust your father, and I know you do, too.

YOUNG NICK
I know it's best, Uncle. I just wish nothing would ever change. I wish we could go back to the way things were. But we can't go back, can we?

NICK'S UNCLE
We can't go back, no. But that doesn't mean we can't take the best of what we've been given along with us wherever we go. The love of your father and mother, that will never leave you... ever.

YOUNG NICK
That's what Father said when Mother died. He said they were one and death couldn't separate

them. He said since she was in heaven now, dancing with Jesus, somehow he felt like he was there, dancing with them, too. Do you believe that, Uncle, that they could still be one even after she died?

NICK'S UNCLE

I do, Nicholas. Just like you're still one with them both, even after your father died. You're truly part of your father and part of your mother, in one new creation. You're still one with them. Do you believe that?

YOUNG NICK

(YOUNG NICK looks at his reflection in a cloudy mirror on the wall)

I do. I just wish I could be with them right now, where they are.

YOUNG NICK bursts into tears and his uncle comforts him.

NICK'S UNCLE

Some day, Nicholas, you will be. It's good to look to the future so you know where you're going. But don't get so caught up in the future that you miss out on what's in front of you today. And today, that means having dinner with me and staying with me for as long as you need. It won't be long, Nicholas, and God will be calling you somewhere else. I'm sure of it. Your mother and father may have died, but you haven't. God still has more for you to do here. Much more.

YOUNG NICK

That's what Father said, too. He said when the plague stops there will be many people who will still need a touch from God. He told me to comfort them with whatever comfort God gives to me. (YOUNG NICK cries again) I just don't see how I can. It hurts so much.

NICK'S UNCLE

I don't know how either of us can, Nicholas. But your father was right. And the same God who gave him strength will give us strength, too.

Upon hearing about his father's strength, Nicholas looks up at the staff leaning against the wall. He stands, crosses the room, and takes hold of it.

NICK'S UNCLE
Ready, Nicholas?

YOUNG NICK
(looking at his staff)
I am now, Uncle. I just have one more stop on our way, if that's all right?

NICK'S UNCLE
Of course. Where would you like to go?

YOUNG NICK
To the sea.

They exit the house as the lights FADE TO BLACK.

ACT 1, SCENE 8 - THE SNOW

YOUNG NICK and NICK'S UNCLE walk near the sea.

NICK'S UNCLE

I'll start climbing the hill, Nicholas. Stay here as long as you'd like, then meet me at the top. You'll make it there much faster than me, anyway.

YOUNG NICK

Thanks, Uncle.

NICK'S UNCLE exits and YOUNG NICK approaches the edge of the sea.

YOUNG NICK

(after a few moments, looking upward)

Dear Lord, I know You said You'd always be with me. And I believe You, I really do. I just wish I could be with You there, just for a little while. You will be with me, right?

He waits for an answer, but hearing none, he speaks, less sure of himself now.

You do remember me, right?

Hearing nothing, he speaks again, in part to himself.

It's Nicholas. Remember?

YOUNG NICK begins to sing.

5. IS THERE ROOM FOR ME?

YOUNG NICK

OH, IS THERE ROOM FOR ME?
OH, IS THERE ROOM FOR ME?
OH, IS THERE ROOM FOR ME,
DEAR LORD, WHERE YOU ARE?

I WON'T BE LONG IN THIS PLACE,
AND I DON'T TAKE UP TOO MUCH SPACE.
I JUST WANT TO SEE YOUR FACE
AND REST INSIDE YOUR WARM EMBRACE.

DO YOU REMEMBER ME?
DO YOU REMEMBER ME?

DO YOU REMEMBER ME,
DEAR LORD, WHERE YOU ARE?

YOUNG NICK looks down, dejected, but then the music changes to a light and airy sound, accompanied by snowflakes that begin to fall gently all around him. YOUNG NICK sees the falling snow and looks up with wonder. The snowfall increases as the music whirls and twirls along with it. Amazed, YOUNG NICK raises his hands toward heaven, feeling the snowflakes in the air as they fall all around him. He smiles a huge smile, then begins to laugh. In that moment, at least, God has turned his mourning into laughter.

With his hands still raised and the snow still falling, the lights FADE TO BLACK.

END OF ACT 1

ACT 2, SCENE 1 - THE CHANCE

Act 2 begins by the sea again, but with three changes: the snow is gone, a ship can be seen off in the distance, and an adult NICHOLAS is now standing in the spot where YOUNG NICK stood before. He's holding the same staff in his hand and is dressed in the same style of clothing so as to be clearly recognizable as an older NICHOLAS. Ten years have passed. NICK'S UNCLE enters and, upon seeing NICHOLAS, angles toward him.

NICK'S UNCLE
Ah, there you are, Nicholas. I knew I'd probably find you here... by the sea.

NICHOLAS
You know I love it here, Uncle! I can always think so much more clearly.

NICK'S UNCLE
(looking out to the sea, then toward the ship in the distance)
I see it's almost here. Still planning to set sail?

NICHOLAS
First thing in the morning, Uncle! As soon as I heard it was coming, I knew I had to be on it. I've been waiting for this day my whole life.

NICK'S UNCLE
And now you're really going to do it, aren't you? You're finally going to the Holy Land.

NICHOLAS
The ship will pass by there and drop me off as it makes its way from Rome to Egypt. Can you imagine, Uncle? To walk where Jesus walked?

NICK'S UNCLE
Your father said that's where you'd head as soon as you were old enough. I can't believe it myself, that this day has finally come.

NICHOLAS

Are you sure you don't want to come with me, Uncle? I've got plenty of money to spare.

NICK'S UNCLE

You certainly do... enough to sail the length of the whole world, back and forth, three or four times, and still have plenty to spare! He was a wise businessman, your father. Prudent in the small things and generous in the big, just like you. But no, I've got things to do here, Nicholas. You, though, have nothing left to keep you here, except me. And I'll be all right. You're young. You're free. Take the chance while you can.

NICHOLAS

Not just "Take the chance," Uncle. "Make the chance." That's what father said. "Dig deep into your heart, Nicholas, and see what God has put inside it. Then go for that."

NICK'S UNCLE

You've always dug deep, Nicholas, that's for sure. And it's clear that God has put something special on your heart. It's one thing to make a living, but quite another to make a life. You're a wise man to take this step.

NICHOLAS

I don't know what the future holds, Uncle, but I know this is the next step God wants me to take. It's as clear as the water in front of me. And isn't that what Jesus said all those years ago? Not to worry about tomorrow, for each day has enough trouble of its own?

NICK'S UNCLE

(looking out, thoughtfully)

He was a wise Man, too, this Jesus. He's always been an enigma to me. Here it is, almost three hundred years since He was born on the other side of the sea, yet His words still make their mark on our hearts today. Humble, yet noble. Born in a stable, yet fed 5,000 in a single meal. He healed so freely, but was killed so cruelly. Yes, He's an enigma. I imagine He's the most fascinating person who's ever lived.

He looks back toward NICHOLAS.

NICK'S UNCLE (CONT'D)
And you're about to walk in His steps.

NICHOLAS looks out across the sea one more time. Then he looks lovingly at his uncle. As he does, he comes to the bittersweet realization that while he's about to take the next big step in his life, he's also about to leave the only family he still has left. NICK'S UNCLE realizes this moment has come, too, the time to say goodbye to his nephew who has grown so close to his heart. NICHOLAS bursts into emotion and embraces his uncle.

NICHOLAS
I'll miss you, dear Uncle.

NICK'S UNCLE
I'll miss you, too, Nicholas. More than you know. More than you know.

FADE TO BLACK.

ACT 2, SCENE 2 - THE LAND

The scene shifts to the Holy Land, where the ship on which NICHOLAS had been sailing has just come ashore. The ship is bustling with activity as ropes are tossed and passengers are disembarking across a simple board which acts as the gangway. People on shore have come to meet the ship with its new arrivals and goods. As NICHOLAS steps across the gangway, he is approached by YOUNG DIMITRI, a boy no more than ten, who is followed somewhat distantly by his two friends, SAMMY and RUTHIE, who are slightly younger than YOUNG DIMITRI.

YOUNG DIMITRI
(tugging at NICHOLAS'S sleeve)
You a Christian?

NICHOLAS looks down to see YOUNG DIMITRI looking up at him.

YOUNG DIMITRI (CONT'D)
You a Christian? I show you holy places?

NICHOLAS
(scanning the scene to make sure it's safe to respond, then...)
Ah, yes, and yes. Yes, I am indeed a Christian. And if you would like to take me, then yes, I would very much like to see the holy places.

NICHOLAS (CONT'D)
(gesturing to YOUNG DIMITRI'S friends)
And I would love for your friends to come along, too. That way if we encounter any trouble, they can defend us all!

YOUNG DIMITRI
(surprised by NICHOLAS'S enthusiastic response, but then quickly recomposing himself, he bows toward NICHOLAS with one hand outstretched, his palm facing upward)
I am Dimitri. Dimitri Alexander.

DIMITRI

(the older storyteller Dimitri pops in briefly from stage left and sits on his stool while all other action on stage stops)

Ah, yes, Dimitri Alexander. That's me! Good looking kid, wasn't I?

All action on stage resumes.

NICHOLAS

(intrigued by YOUNG DIMITRI'S posture, which suggests either "I'm at your service" or "You can tip me now")

Well, Dimitri Alexander, I am Nicholas. Nicholas of Patara, and I am very pleased to make your acquaintance.

NICHOLAS reaches into his pocket and pulls out three small coins to place into YOUNG DIMITRI'S outstretched hand.

NICHOLAS (CONT'D)

There's one, there's two, and there's three.

YOUNG DIMITRI'S mouth drops open as he looks in his hand, not at the size of the coins but at the generous spirit with which they were given. He begins to clasp his hand around the coins when NICHOLAS interrupts him.

NICHOLAS (CONT'D)

And I can see you're a very wise man. Now, if you're able to keep your hand open even after receiving these coins, you'll be even wiser still. For he who clenches his fist tightly around that which he has received will find it hard to receive more. But he who opens his hand toward heaven, freely giving as he has freely received, will find that his Father in heaven will rarely hold back from giving him more.

NICHOLAS motions with his hand toward YOUNG DIMITRI'S two friends, indicating that YOUNG DIMITRI might want to share with them what he has received. YOUNG DIMITRI considers this, looking from the coins in his hand to the smile on NICHOLAS'S face. YOUNG DIMITRI unclenches his fist and offers its contents to his friends.

Seizing the opportunity, both SAMMY and RUTHIE quickly reach into YOUNG DIMITRI'S hand, pulling out one coin each, then clasping their hands tightly around the coins, just as YOUNG DIMITRI had done. Catching what they were doing, and NICHOLAS'S smile, SAMMY and RUTHIE unclench their hands, holding their palms upward, just as YOUNG DIMITRI is still doing.

Delighted by their response, NICHOLAS reaches into his pocket again, pulls out six more coins, and places two more coins into each child's hand, one coin at a time, mouthing the words silently to each child, "There's two and there's three." Again, the THREE CHILDREN are caught off guard by this generosity, and they look back and forth between the coins and NICHOLAS'S face.

Seeing the sight of the three of them, standing there with their hands still outstretched and amazement on their faces, NICHOLAS bursts into a genuine laugh.

NICHOLAS

Now you'd better close your hands again because a wise man... or woman... (nodding toward RUTHIE) also takes care of what they've been given so it doesn't get lost or stolen.

NICHOLAS (CONT'D)

(looking around and then to YOUNG DIMITRI)

And if you could point me toward Straight Street, I hear there's an inn where I can get some rest until I get my land legs back.

All THREE CHILDREN raise their free hands and point in the same direction.

NICHOLAS (CONT'D)

(looking where they are pointing)

How about you meet me there first thing in the morning, then you can start showing me those holy places?

NICHOLAS bows to the children, who return his bow then run off with their coins in their hands and delight on their faces.

NICHOLAS (CONT'D)

(looking toward heaven)

Holy places. They want to show me holy places. But I think I've just seen the first one... right here.

The music begins.

6. HERE I STAND

Sensing the holiness of the moment, NICHOLAS takes off his shoes, standing and feeling the soil with his bare feet... the soil of this most Holy Place.

NICHOLAS

HERE I STAND
IN THIS HOLY LAND,
STANDING HAND IN HAND
WITH THE GREAT "I AM!"

BUT WHAT MAKES IT SO HOLY
IS NOT WHERE THIS PLACE IS.
IT'S THE TOUCH OF YOUR HAND,
IT'S THE LOOKS ON THEIR FACES.
I DIDN'T KNOW HOW
I SHOULD ANSWER THE QUESTION,
IF I WAS OR WAS NOT
TRULY DEEP DOWN A CHRISTIAN.
YET YOU KNEW WHAT I NEEDED
RIGHT NOW WAS A GUIDE,
FOR THE MONEY I'VE GOT,
BUT A MAP I DO NOT.
THEN I LOOKED AT HIS SMILE
WITH HIS HAND OPENED WIDE,
AND I SAID IN MY HEART,
"YES! THE LORD WILL PROVIDE!"

SO HERE I STAND
IN THIS HOLY LAND,
STANDING HAND IN HAND
WITH THE GREAT "I AM!"

NOW THEY SAY THEY WILL SHOW ME
THE MOST HOLY PLACES.
WHAT I COULDN'T IMAGINE
AND NOW CAN'T ERASE IS
THE MOST HOLY PLACES
ARE THOSE WHERE YOUR GRACE IS,
WHERE HEAVEN AND EARTH
ARE NO LONGER TWO SPACES,
WHERE THE VEIL THAT'S BETWEEN THEM'S
SO UTTERLY THIN,
THAT I SWEAR I COULD PRACTICALLY
TAKE A PEAK IN,
WHERE I SENSE IN AN INSTANT
YOUR PRESENCE SO CEARLY,

TO KNOW THAT YOU LOVE ME
MOST TRULY AND DEARLY!

NOW HERE I STAND
IN THIS HOLY LAND,
STANDING HAND IN HAND
WITH THE GREAT "I AM!"

HERE I STAND!

NICHOLAS takes a final look toward heaven, nods, and then sets off in the direction the children pointed to the inn. The lights FADE TO BLACK.

ACT 2, SCENE 3 - THE CHILDREN

The sun rises over Joppa on stage left while a knock at NICHOLAS'S door to his room, stage right, alerts him to the fact that the children have arrived. NICHOLAS opens the door, refreshed from the night.

NICHOLAS
Right on time! Ready to go?

YOUNG DIMITRI
Yes, sir! Where to, first?

NICHOLAS
I thought we'd start at the beginning, in Bethlehem, the place where Jesus was born.

YOUNG DIMITRI
Bethlehem?!? That's a three-day walk!

NICHOLAS
Three days, really? Well, maybe we'd better start closer to home. Your families wouldn't want you to go so far on such short notice.

YOUNG DIMITRI
(looking hesitantly at SAMMY and RUTHIE)
We... don't have any families, sir. It's just us.

RUTHIE
He's right. We're alumni. Orphans. None of us ever knew our parents. But practically speaking, *we're* a family.

She beams and nods toward YOUNG DIMITRI and SAMMY.

YOUNG DIMITRI
I found Sammy and Ruthie a few years back, and we've stuck together ever since. They looked like they needed some help, and, well, I was glad to have a few friends myself.

SAMMY
(putting his arm around YOUNG DIMITRI and beaming along with RUTHIE)
We're practically brothers, right?

RUTHIE

So there's no need to worry about us. We can go whenever you're ready.

NICHOLAS

(pausing momentarily to assess if they're telling the truth, then deciding they are)

I see. I knew my parents, but I lost them when I was young, too. God helped me through it, just like I know He'll help you. (in a more upbeat tone) And I see you are indeed ready. Let's start at the beginning then, shall we? But three days? We'll need some supplies to take a journey that long. (grabbing his sack and putting in a few of his belongings) If you'll show me where we can buy some food for the trip, we'll stock up before heading out.

YOUNG DIMITRI

(bowing and holding out his hand as he had done the night before)

At your service.

NICHOLAS

(taking YOUNG DIMITRI'S hand and shaking it this time, instead of giving him a coin)

And I am at yours. How about I buy you a treat for breakfast today? What kind of fruit do you like?

YOUNG DIMITRI

Oranges!

SAMMY

And lemons!

RUTHIE

And limes!

NICHOLAS

(smiling)

Oh my! (pause) That sounds delicious! Show me where to find them, and we'll make a feast of it!

NICHOLAS throws his bag over his shoulder and, taking his staff in hand, follows the children as they rush out the door. The entire room is whisked off stage right, revealing an early morning marketplace in Joppa. Street merchants are selling bread and cheese, fish and meat, fruit and vegetables. The market is abuzz with buyers and sellers. Talking and laughing and greetings fill the fresh morning air.

YOUNG DIMITRI
(waving from the orange seller's stand)
Over here!

NICHOLAS looks and starts to head in that direction but then hears SAMMY'S voice.

SAMMY
(waving from the lemon seller's stand)
Over here!

NICHOLAS looks toward him but then hears RUTHIE'S voice.

RUTHIE
(waving from the lime seller's stand)
Over here!

NICHOLAS gives a laugh, and the THREE CHILDREN burst into song. He joins them in singing as do the rest of the ADULTS and CHILDREN in the marketplace.

7. ORANGES AND LEMONS AND LIMES

YOUNG DIMITRI
I FOUND SOME ORANGES HERE!

SAMMY
I FOUND SOME LEMONS THERE!

RUTHIE
I FOUND SOME LIMES RIGHT HERE,
AND I'LL BE GLAD TO SHARE!

NICHOLAS
WE'RE GOING TO TAKE A TRIP,
SEE WHERE IT ALL BEGAN.

ALL FOUR
WE'RE GOING TO WALK, WALK, WALK, WALK,
WALK THREE DAYS UNTIL WE'RE THERE!

YOUNG DIMITRI

(to himself)

WHO IS THIS MAN?
WHY DOES HE CARE?

SAMMY

(to himself)

WHAT WILL WE DO
WHEN WE GET THERE?

RUTHIE

(to herself)

I'M NOT SURE WHAT
THIS DAY MIGHT BRING.
IT COULD BE
ALMOST ANYTHING!
CATCH ME IF YOU DARE!

All three run to different vendors.

YOUNG DIMITRI

I FOUND SOME BREAD RIGHT HERE!

SAMMY

THERE'S FETA CHEESE RIGHT THERE!

RUTHIE

I FOUND SOME SPICES HERE.
I THINK THIS PRICE IS FAIR!

NICHOLAS

WE'RE GOING TO TAKE A TRIP,
SEE WHERE IT ALL BEGAN.

ALL

(running in place)

WE'RE GOING TO RUN, RUN, RUN, RUN,
RUN THREE DAYS UNTIL WE'RE THERE!

YOUNG DIMITRI

(to himself)

COULD THIS BE WHAT
REAL FAITH LOOKS LIKE?

SAMMY

I HOPE DIMITRI
GUIDES US RIGHT!

RUTHIE

IT FEELS SO GOOD
I'VE GOT TO SING!
THIS DAY COULD BRING
US ANYTHING!
CATCH ME IF YOU DARE!

YOUNG DIMITRI

I FOUND SOME YOGURT HERE!

SAMMY

THERE'S POMEGRANATE THERE!

RUTHIE

I FOUND SOME HYSSOP HERE.
IT GOES WITH CHICKEN THERE!

NICHOLAS

(the THREE CHILDREN climb onto his and each other's backs)

WE'RE GOING TO TAKE A TRIP,
SEE WHERE IT ALL BEGAN.

ALL

WE'RE GOING TO RIDE, RIDE, RIDE, RIDE,
RIDE THREE DAYS UNTIL WE'RE THERE!

YOUNG DIMITRI

I WONDER WHAT
WE'LL LEARN OUT THERE?

SAMMY

I FEEL A CHANGE
IS IN THE AIR.

RUTHIE

(jumping onto some boxes to get higher)

MY HEART IS DOING
CRAZY THINGS!
I FEEL LIKE I'VE
BEEN GIVEN WINGS!

ALL

(RUTHIE dives off the boxes and crowd surfs over the heads of the people in the marketplace)

CATCH ME IF YOU DARE!

During a brief musical interlude, everyone forms two or three kick lines and sings together.

ALL (CONT'D)

I FOUND SOME ORANGES HERE!
I FOUND SOME LEMONS THERE!
I FOUND SOME LIMES RIGHT HERE,
AND I'LL BE GLAD TO SHARE!
WE'RE GOING TO TAKE A TRIP,
SEE WHERE IT ALL BEGAN.

(making walking motions)

WE'RE GOING TO WALK, WALK, WALK, WALK,
WALK THREE DAYS UNTIL WE'RE THERE!

Everyone strikes a final pose. A reprise of the song begins as the buyers and sellers all go back to their business and NICHOLAS and the THREE CHILDREN take off on theirs. As they go, the music fades, and the lights FADE TO BLACK.

ACT 2, SCENE 4 - THE QUESTIONS

NICHOLAS and the THREE CHILDREN walk through a grassy hillside. All of them are visibly worn out after two days of walking, running, and riding on each other's backs on their way to Bethlehem. They're singing, but it's taking all the strength they've got.

SAMMY
(dragging both his feet and his voice)
We're going to walk, walk, walk, walk,
walk three days until we're there...

YOUNG DIMITRI
Two days down, one to go, Sammy. Come on, Ruthie, catch up!

RUTHIE
(trailing behind the rest)
I'd be fine, except I have to take two steps for every one of yours. So mathematically, *I've* been walking four days, not two.

NICHOLAS
I think this looks like a good spot to take a break. What do you think?

All three kids drop to the ground with relief.

NICHOLAS (CONT'D)
I'll take that as a "Yes."

NICHOLAS sits on a nearby rock as the THREE CHILDREN scoot closer. NICHOLAS pulls out a loaf of bread from his sack and passes it around as they all tear off a chunk to eat. While eating, they converse. YOUNG DIMITRI leans back on the rock, looking at the sky.

YOUNG DIMITRI
(to NICHOLAS)
Why do you think He did it? I mean, why would Jesus want to come here, to earth? If I were in heaven, I think I'd want to stay there.

SAMMY
You're the guide, Dimitri. Don't you know?

YOUNG DIMITRI

(to SAMMY, while nodding to NICHOLAS)

But I've never guided someone like him before. I figure I'd better ask all the questions I can while I can.

NICHOLAS

And I don't mind answering them, at least whenever I have the answers. I used to ask my father questions like this all the time, just like you're asking me.

YOUNG DIMITRI

So why did He do it? Why *did* Jesus leave heaven and come down to earth?

NICHOLAS

It's because, well, some things have to be done in person. We already knew God loved us. He didn't have to come here to tell us that. Look around at everything He's created for us to enjoy! Sunlight and food and colors and textures and sounds!

But for all the good He's done for us, *we* don't always do what's good for us. Sometimes we do things that hurt Him or hurt others or hurt ourselves. And oftentimes we can't undo those hurts alone.

So Jesus came to undo them for us, paying the price with His life for everything we've ever done wrong. That way we could come back to God by putting our faith in Him, getting a clean slate and a clean heart so we can live with Him forever, even after our lives here on earth are over.

YOUNG DIMITRI

(thinking)

I've been to Bethlehem and other holy places many times, but I've never heard these things explained the way you explain them. It's all starting to make sense now.

NICHOLAS

I think sometimes life gets in the way of our ability to hear God... to really hear Him... and what He's trying to say to us. I suppose it might have been easier for me to hear God because I grew up with people who always told me how very much God loved me and how very much they loved me. It sure got harder once they were gone.

NICHOLAS pulls out some apples and hands one to each of them.

NICHOLAS (CONT'D)

And that's what He wants us to do for others... to show them how very much He loves them and how very much we love them so they can believe in Him, too.

The kids look at NICHOLAS as each of their own barriers to faith are visibly coming down. They begin to eat their apples.

RUTHIE

Why Bethlehem? Why not someplace more important, like Jerusalem or Rome or Alexandria?

NICHOLAS

What looks important to God doesn't always look important to us. He chose Bethlehem because of someone who lived there about 1,000 years before Jesus was born.

SAMMY

King David, right?

NICHOLAS

That's right, Sammy! And even though David didn't do everything right, he always came back to God and tried to make things right with Him. And for that, God wanted to do something special to honor him. God is always on the lookout to do something special for those whose hearts are fully committed to Him.

RUTHIE

Would He do something special for me?

NICHOLAS

Of course He would, Ruthie! And He already has.

(nodding toward YOUNG DIMITRI and SAMMY)

RUTHIE

(thinking again)

What if I ask Him for something, and He doesn't answer my prayers?

NICHOLAS

Oh, He always answers your prayers, Ruthie. Sometimes with a "Yes," sometimes with a "No," and sometimes with a "Not yet." But He always answers in a way that's best for you in the end.

RUTHIE

(after digesting these words for a moment)

I like the way you think. I believe you.

She stands up again.

RUTHIE (CONT'D)

I'm ready to go now. My legs are filled up with strength again. But I'm going to get a head start because I have to take twice as many steps as you!

She sprints off.

SAMMY

(jumping up to catch her)

You won't beat me!

YOUNG DIMITRI

(standing up with NICHOLAS)

Looks like I just lost my job as a guide.

NICHOLAS

Not at all, Dimitri. I think you may be just getting started.

With a wink to YOUNG DIMITRI and a look to heaven, NICHOLAS and YOUNG DIMITRI walk off in the direction of SAMMY and RUTHIE as the lights FADE TO BLACK.

ACT 2, SCENE 5 - THE GIFTS

As evening approaches on the third day, NICHOLAS and the THREE CHILDREN walk up the final hill to Bethlehem.

YOUNG DIMITRI

(pointing ahead)

There it is! That hill up ahead with the cave carved into the side of it! That's the stable where the animals were kept in the days of Jesus.

SAMMY

That's where Jesus was born!

RUTHIE

You *were* right, Dimitri! We *did* make it in three days!

YOUNG DIMITRI

See that path leading up to the cave? That's the path we're headed for.

NICHOLAS

(looking in awe at the path ahead)

I can't believe I'm really here! I've wanted to see this place my whole life. Is it safe to go on the path?

YOUNG DIMITRI

I've never had any trouble before. Even though it's against the law to worship anyone but Caesar, pilgrims come here all the time, and the Romans don't seem to enforce that law as much way out here.

NICHOLAS

Then let's get to the path! I can't wait.

All of them run ahead to the path that leads to their destination. It's a narrow, but well-worn route to the cave, having had thousands of pilgrims traversing it over the years. After a short time on the path, NICHOLAS stops and lets out a laugh. The children stop to look at him.

NICHOLAS

I was just thinking of the wise men who came to Bethlehem to see Jesus. They may have come up this very same path. How regal they must have looked, riding their camels and bringing their gifts of gold and frankincense and myrrh.

SAMMY

I've ridden a camel!

NICHOLAS

Well, for a moment there I pictured myself riding a camel, too, just like one of those kings. But then I stepped in some sheep dung. The smell reminded me I'm not riding a camel, and I'm certainly not royalty!

RUTHIE

(thinking)

But smelling like sheep dung might make you more like the shepherds who saw Jesus that night he was born. And they got there first!

NICHOLAS

You're absolutely right, Ruthie!

RUTHIE smiles at her insight, but then her face becomes thoughtful again.

RUTHIE

Maybe we should bring a gift with us, too, like the wise men did?

The thought overtakes her, as if she's truly concerned that she has nothing to give to honor Jesus. She looks around, then spots some golden flowers on the hillside.

RUTHIE (CONT'D)

(pointing)

Look!

She leaves the path and picks four small flowers, then returns and hands one to each of them.

RUTHIE (CONT'D)

They look like gold to me!

RUTHIE smiles from ear to ear, and NICHOLAS can't help but smile with her.

NICHOLAS

They certainly do, Ruthie. There's always something you can give, isn't there? Whether gold from a mine or golden flowers from a hillside, everything we have comes from God anyway, doesn't it?

They continue walking as NICHOLAS looks at his flower and begins to sing.

8. THERE'S ALWAYS SOMETHING YOU CAN GIVE

NICHOLAS

THERE'S ALWAYS SOMETHING YOU CAN GIVE.
LOOK AROUND AND YOU WILL SEE,
WHETHER GOLD OR GOLDEN FLOWERS THAT LIVE
ON THE HILLS BENEATH YOUR FEET.

EVEN THOUGH WE KNOW
ALL THINGS COME FROM ABOVE,
STILL THERE'S NO GREATER SHOW
OF OUR HEARTS THAN TO GIVE IN LOVE.

THERE'S ALWAYS SOMETHING YOU CAN GIVE.
LOOK INSIDE AND YOU WILL SEE
THAT YOUR HEART IS WHERE TRUE BLESSINGS LIVE.
WHAT A GIFT TRUE LOVE CAN BE!

EVEN THOUGH WE KNOW
ALL THINGS COME FROM ABOVE,
STILL THERE'S NO GREATER SHOW
OF OUR HEARTS THAN TO GIVE IN LOVE.

As the song ends, they reach the entrance to the cave. The THREE CHILDREN look at one another, then to NICHOLAS, motioning for him to go inside first. NICHOLAS lights a small lamp and ducks inside, followed by the THREE CHILDREN, as the lights FADE TO BLACK.

ACT 2, SCENE 6 - THE OFFERING

As NICHOLAS enters the cave, the light from his lamp reveals a solitary wooden manger and a star etched into the floor beside it.

YOUNG DIMITRI

(pointing to the manger)

This manger was put here by some pilgrims who came before us as a reminder of the manger that baby Jesus slept in. And that star next to it, etched into the ground, everyone touches it when they come here so they can touch the hillside where Jesus was born.

NICHOLAS

(amazed)

To think that God made His entrance into the world as a Man *right here*. A Man who healed the sick, walked on water, and raised the dead. A Man who spoke with authority because He was the Author of life. And to think He not only came to this spot, but that He came to us at all.

RUTHIE

Your parents must have loved Him, and you, very much to tell you so many stories about Him.

NICHOLAS

They did, Ruthie. They loved Him so much they were willing to give up their lives to serve Him to the end. (smiling again) I can't believe I'm really here! I know this is just a place, just a spot on the ground. But still, the idea that Jesus was born here, in Bethlehem!

NICHOLAS is suddenly overcome with emotion. He drops to his knees in front of the manger and bows his head to the ground. Seeing him kneel, the THREE CHILDREN follow suit, two on one side of him and one on the other. After a pause, NICHOLAS raises his head and looks around.

NICHOLAS

I feel like there's something I should do or say. I've always believed in Jesus, but somehow I want to commit my life to Him here in a special way. I feel like I have more faith in

Him now than I've ever had in my life. But I'm not sure what I'm supposed to do?

Ruthie looks at Nicholas and holds up her flower. Then he remembers. Lifting his hand and holding the flower in front of him, he gazes at it lovingly. It's no longer just a flower, but an offering of his entire life to his Savior.

NICHOLAS

(thinking aloud)

There's always something you can give, isn't there?

NICHOLAS leans forward once again and lays the flower on the ground in front of the manger. When he does, each of the THREE CHILDREN slowly do the same, offering their flowers and their lives to God. The music begins to play with an instrumental reprise of the song NICHOLAS just sang.

9. THERE'S ALWAYS SOMETHING YOU CAN GIVE (REPRISE)

When the song shifts to a higher key, an offstage choir sings the words again, giving the song and the mood a palpable lift.

CHOIR

THERE'S ALWAYS SOMETHING YOU CAN GIVE.
LOOK AROUND AND YOU WILL SEE,
WHETHER GOLD OR GOLDEN FLOWERS THAT LIVE
ON THE HILLS BENEATH YOUR FEET.

EVEN THOUGH WE KNOW
ALL THINGS COME FROM ABOVE,
STILL THERE'S NO GREATER SHOW
OF OUR HEARTS THAN TO GIVE IN LOVE.

As the choir sings, several tableaus light up around the stage, one after another, each showing people giving various gifts. A girl draws a picture at a table then hands her artwork to her mother, a boy unwraps a package that's been given to him by a friend, a man gives a coin to another man, a woman hands a plateful of food to another woman who receives it gratefully, and a little child gives an orange to another child, just as NICHOLAS and NICK'S FATHER had done earlier. The song reaches its climax when EVERYONE on stage joins the CHOIR in singing. As the song ends, the lights FADE TO BLACK.

END OF ACT 2

ACT 3, SCENE 1 - THE DEPARTURE

NICHOLAS stands at the edge of the sea at the same spot where he first landed in the Holy Land. This time as he looks out over the water, a large cargo ship from Alexandria is docked in the port. NICHOLAS glances over his shoulder toward the street behind him as the SHIP'S CAPTAIN approaches from the other direction.

SHIP'S CAPTAIN
No sign of your friends yet?

NICHOLAS
No sign. Either they didn't get the message or they couldn't make it. I did hope I'd be able to say goodbye.

SHIP'S CAPTAIN
What's your hurry? You said you've been here for four years already. What's so important that you have to leave now?

NICHOLAS
It's... hard to explain. Do you believe in God?

SHIP'S CAPTAIN
I've been a captain on this sea for thirty years. A man would have to be a little bit crazy to sail these waters and *not* believe in God.

NICHOLAS
Then maybe it's not so hard to explain after all. I feel like God's been telling me it's time. Time to go home. Time to get back to the other side of the sea where I'm from. I came here to walk where Jesus walked, and I've done that for four years now. But I know I've got to get back. I thought I missed my chance last week when the last ship pulled out of the harbor before the winter storms. But when you showed up this morning, I knew I hadn't missed it at all, that God *had* been speaking to me, and that *your* ship was the one that I needed to take.

SHIP'S CAPTAIN
I'm glad you think it's divinely appointed because we should have been here and gone a week ago, too. Do you really think it is... divinely appointed?

NICHOLAS
I know it is. God's been speaking to me lately in a way that's crystal clear.

SHIP'S CAPTAIN
(looking surprised)
You mean He talked to you, like I'm talking to you now?

NICHOLAS
(laughing)
Oh, no! It was much louder than that.

SHIP'S CAPTAIN
(laughing, then thinking)
These holy places you talked about... what did you see?

NICHOLAS
What did we see? How could I describe these last four years? We went to the cave in Bethlehem where Jesus was born. We swam in the Sea of Galilee where Jesus walked on water. We picnicked on the hill where He fed 5,000 with two fish and five loaves of bread. We knelt at the spot in Jerusalem where He suffered and died. And we stood at the empty tomb where He rose again from the dead.

NICHOLAS looks at the SHIP'S CAPTAIN and notices he is eyeing him carefully.

NICHOLAS (CONT'D)
But that's not what you're asking, is it? You're asking if we saw *Him*, aren't you? I can tell you, most assuredly, we saw Him everywhere we looked.

SHIP'S CAPTAIN
I've heard tell that those who seek Him find Him, and that some people have found Him here. You've just confirmed it to me.

NICHOLAS

Some people live here day in and day out and never see what we've seen because they're not looking with the eyes God has given to us.

SHIP'S CAPTAIN

What eyes are those?

NICHOLAS

The eyes of a *Believer*. I can tell you've got those eyes. You've seen Him, haven't you?

SHIP'S CAPTAIN

I have. But not here. Only when I'm out at sea. I've felt Him come to me, but I haven't known what to do. What to say. What do you say when the God of the universe shows up in your boat?

NICHOLAS

I say, "Welcome. Come on in. Say whatever You want to say. Let me know whatever you want me to do. And if there's nothing special You want to say or want me to do, then just know how happy I am that You want to be with me for a while." That's what I say.

SHIP'S CAPTAIN

And what does He say?

NICHOLAS

The same thing! "Welcome. Come on in. Say whatever you want to say. Let Me know whatever you want Me to do. And if there's nothing special you want to say or want Me to do, then just know how happy I am that you want to be with Me for a while." That's what He says!

SHIP'S CAPTAIN

He says all of that to you?

NICHOLAS

Well, not always in so many words. But yes, that's what He says, quite often. And know this, no matter who you are or what you've done, He says the same to you. "Welcome. Come on in. I'm happy to have You be with Me for a while."

SHIP’S CAPTAIN

(thinking again)

I’m glad you’re coming along. I have a feeling we’ll need a man like you on this trip. We leave first thing in the morning or we might not be able to leave till spring. I do hope your friends make it in time to say goodbye.

NICHOLAS

So do I.

The SHIP'S CAPTAIN and NICHOLAS look out over the sea again.

NICHOLAS (CONT’D)

So do I.

FADE TO BLACK.

ACT 3, SCENE 2 - THE FAREWELL

The morning sun lights up the stage as the SHIP'S CAPTAIN, now on board, calls out commands to his CREW MATES to prepare to leave. NICHOLAS stands, still alone, on the shore.

SHIP'S CAPTAIN
Storm's picking up, Nicholas! We've got to go.

NICHOLAS looks back one more time and sighs with resignation, then heads toward the ship. Just before he gets to the gangplank, DIMITRI sneaks up behind him and tugs on his sleeve just as he did the first time they met. SAMMY and RUTHIE approach from further back, out of breath.

YOUNG DIMITRI
You a Christian?

NICHOLAS
(wheeling around and seeing all THREE CHILDREN)
Am I a Christian? Without a doubt! And you?

YOUNG DIMITRI, SAMMY, AND RUTHIE
(nearly in unison)
Without a doubt!

NICHOLAS
Any doubts we had about our faith faded that day in Bethlehem, didn't they? Hold out your hands!

The THREE CHILDREN know what's coming, so they look at NICHOLAS and each other reluctantly. They're not as young anymore, and they don't need the money as they did before, either. But because it's NICHOLAS, they smile at him and each hold out their right hands.

NICHOLAS reaches into his pocket and pulls out three of his largest coins. But before he can put them in their hands, they rush forward and wrap their arms around his neck, back, and waist, according to their height, holding on tight. Then they break apart and look at each other with tears in their eyes.

RUTHIE
I'm sorry for crying. I know you have to go. I just wish you didn't.

NICHOLAS

I wish I didn't, too. But the same Spirit who led me here is leading me home again, with an even stronger pull this time. And about the crying, no need to be sorry. Remember, tears are one of the greatest signs of love you can ever give to anyone.

NICHOLAS hugs RUTHIE, and she cries again.

NICHOLAS (CONT'D)

Knowing God's will doesn't always mean it's easy to do. But we can always trust Him. Always. He always knows best.

SHIP'S CAPTAIN

Last call, Nicholas! We're pulling out!

SAMMY

You're the best, Nicholas! Your presents were great, but your *presence* is best. We'll miss you. Now all I have left are these two to follow around.

NICHOLAS hugs SAMMY.

YOUNG DIMITRI

(holding back his own tears)

Will we ever see you again?

NICHOLAS

We're Believers, aren't we? For Believers it's never "goodbye for good" only "goodbye for now." So, "Goodbye for now." Your hugs and tears will carry me through whatever's next.

All three hug him again, tighter than before. As they do, NICHOLAS looks to heaven and finally slips a large coin into each of their pockets. He smiles as he does, knowing they'll find them later.

The final refrain plays again of "There's Always Something You Can Give" as the lights FADE TO BLACK.

ACT 3, SCENE 3 - THE STORM

The ship pulls out and the dock fades into the distance. After getting the ship underway, the SHIP'S CAPTAIN finds NICHOLAS again on its bow.

NICHOLAS
Outrunning this storm is as crazy as outrunning winter itself, isn't it?

SHIP'S CAPTAIN
If I thought we had a choice, I would have waited till spring. But outrunning this storm is our best chance to beat the drought back in Rome.

NICHOLAS
The drought?

SHIP'S CAPTAIN
You really have been gone a while, haven't you? That's why we've got to keep this ship moving, all the way around the coast, until we get to Rome. We've had rain down here on the southern coast, but up north the famine's spreading like wildfire. I wish we didn't have to go around the coast to get there, but traveling straight across the sea at this time of year is out of the question.

NICHOLAS
(sensing anxiousness in the SHIP'S CAPTAIN)
Your hurry isn't just about getting this grain to Caesar, is it?

SHIP'S CAPTAIN
(unsure if he should answer, but then speaking as he senses he can trust NICHOLAS)
Half the crew and their families are from Rome, including mine. If we don't get this grain there soon, we'll lose more than just time.

NICHOLAS
(to himself)
Storm or no storm, we've got to go on.

SHIP'S CAPTAIN
I'm sorry?

NICHOLAS
I said, "Storm or no storm, we've got to go on." This urgency I've felt about getting back home, it's making more sense to me now. I've been feeling it for a few months. At first it was just a restlessness, a growing discontent with staying here. I had no reason to leave. I was happy here. But then...

SHIP'S CAPTAIN
...you knew you had to go, didn't you? You knew the time had come? I've felt that before. I feel it now. It's like...

NICHOLAS
...you couldn't stay put if you tried.

SHIP'S CAPTAIN
How did you know where to go? That restlessness told you *when*, but how did you know *where*?

NICHOLAS
I've found the biggest obstacle to knowing God's will is knowing when to let go of your own... or at least making sure your will isn't standing in the way of His. I came to the point where I was willing to go anywhere He called me, to do anything He wanted me to do. Then it came to me. It was time to go home. There was a reason I was born where I was, when I was, and I knew it was time to go back.

SHIP'S CAPTAIN
So storm or no storm, you've got to go on.

NICHOLAS
Storm or no storm, so do you.

A bolt of lightning streaks across the sky as the music swells. NICHOLAS and the SHIP'S CAPTAIN turn their faces toward the wind and begin to sing.

10. STORM OR NO STORM

NICHOLAS

SOMETHING'S STIRRING IN THE AIR TONIGHT,
I CAN FEEL IT ALL AROUND.

SHIP'S CAPTAIN

SOMETHING'S STIRRING IN MY SOUL ALL RIGHT,
I CAN FEEL MY HEARTBEAT POUND.

NICHOLAS

AND I KNOW WHERE'ER I GO
YOU WILL GO SO I WON'T FEAR.

SHIP'S CAPTAIN

AND I KNOW WHERE'ER I GO
YOU WILL GUIDE ME LOUD AND CLEAR.

NICHOLAS

STORM OR NO STORM,
THE SPIRIT SAYS GO,
SO LET IT BLOW!

SHIP'S CAPTAIN

STORM OR NO STORM,
MY SPIRIT SAYS GO,
SO LET IT BLOW!

TOGETHER

OH, O-OH, O-OH!

ALL

SOMETHING'S STIRRING IN THE AIR TONIGHT,
I CAN FEEL IT ALL AROUND.
SOMETHING'S STIRRING IN MY SOUL ALL RIGHT,
I CAN FEEL MY HEARTBEAT POUND.

AND I KNOW WHERE'ER I GO
YOU WILL GO SO I WON'T FEAR.
AND I KNOW WHERE'ER I GO
YOU WILL GUIDE ME LOUD AND CLEAR.

STORM OR NO STORM,
THE SPIRIT SAYS GO,
SO LET IT BLOW!

STORM OR NO STORM,
MY SPIRIT SAYS GO,
SO LET IT BLOW!

OH, O-OH, O-OH!

The wind blows strong, whipping their hair, as the lights FADE TO BLACK.

ACT 3, SCENE 4 - THE SONG

The same ship, three days later. NICHOLAS, the SHIP'S CAPTAIN, and several CREW MATES are on deck, including a YOUNG SHIPMATE, all of whom are seasick and drenched as waves continue to break over the lurching ship.

NICHOLAS
(loudly, over the waves)
I thought it was bad after three hours, but three days?!? And still no sign of letting up!

SHIP'S CAPTAIN
(just as loudly)
If someone had told me before we left we'd be this far out to sea, I wouldn't have believed them. But we had no choice. We had to let go of the rudder and go with the storm or we'd have been blasted apart by the waves. I pray we can make it through another day.

NICHOLAS
I pray we can make it through another hour!

YOUNG SHIPMATE
I pray we can make it through another wave!

All three are tossed to one side of the ship as they're pelted by another wave. As the wave subsides, they regain their composure.

NICHOLAS
I've tried to remember what the Apostle Paul did when he made a trip across this sea in a storm like this. Luke wrote about it in one of stories, saying it lasted for 14 days before they got shipwrecked on the island of Malta.

From what I recall, an angel showed up to Paul one night telling him to take heart, that even though the ship would be destroyed not one of the men traveling with him would perish... and there were 276 of them! Paul believed the angel, and everything happened just as he said.

YOUNG SHIPMATE
(hopefully)
Has an angel appeared to you?

NICHOLAS shakes his heads "No." The YOUNG SHIPMATE looks at the SHIP'S CAPTAIN who also shakes his head "No."

YOUNG SHIPMATE (CONT'D)
(downcast)
Me either. What are we going to do?

Any veneer of toughness or hope that the YOUNG SHIPMATE had disappears as yet another wave breaks over the side of the ship. He holds on tight, then breaks down in tears.

NICHOLAS
All I know is that God told me before we left that I *had* to get home as soon as I could. I know it's hard to hang on to Jesus when the winds are howling like this... about as hard as hanging on to that slippery mast. But there's nothing else I'd rather hang on to than Him. And the truth is, even if we can't hang on anymore, He'll still hang on to us.

The YOUNG SHIPMATE looks to NICHOLAS with desperate hope, wanting to believe him but unsure if he can. After a pause, NICHOLAS continues.

NICHOLAS
My father once told me that "standing orders are good orders." If a soldier wasn't sure what to do next, no matter how fierce the battle grew around them, then the last orders were to be carried out in full. "Standing orders are good orders."

The YOUNG SHIPMATE and the SHIP'S CAPTAIN are now giving NICHOLAS their full attention.

NICHOLAS (CONT'D)
I think we're in that place now. It's that one piece of wisdom from my father, more than anything else, that makes me think we're in the center of God's will... even if it feels like we're in the center of a hurricane.

With another lurch of the ship, NICHOLAS, the YOUNG SHIPMATE, and the SHIP'S CAPTAIN hang on even tighter to the ship's mast. The

YOUNG SHIPMATE begins to rise from where he had fallen at the base of the mast to stand next to NICHOLAS and the SHIP'S CAPTAIN. Magically and mystically, the storm begins to transform into a slow-motion version of itself as NICHOLAS begins to sing.

11. HE'S THE SONG

NICHOLAS

(tenderly)

THERE'S A STILL, SMALL VOICE
THAT INSTILLS GREAT PEACE,
AND IT GIVES ME CHEER
TO MAKE MY RELEASE;
LETTING GO OF ALL
THAT WOULD HOLD ME BACK,
TO TAKE HOLD OF HIM
WHO KNOWS NO LACK.

STAY THE COURSE,
HOLD ON TIGHT,
LET THE DARK
BE CAST OUT BY HIS LIGHT.

HE'S THE CALM,
HE'S THE CALM,
HE'S THE CALM
IN THE RAGING OF THE SEA.

HE'S THE CALM,
HE'S THE CALM,
HE'S THE CALM
WHO COMFORTS ME.

I COULD WRITE A SONG
OF HIS LOVE FOR ME,
HOW HE LIVED AND DIED,
GAVE HIS LIFE FOR ME.
BUT I'VE HEARD THAT HE
WROTE A SONG FOR ME,
AND THE SONG HE SINGS
IS BOTH WILD AND FREE.

STAY THE COURSE,
DON'T YOU POUT,
LET HIS SONG
DRIVE THE DARKNESS OUT.

HE'S THE SONG,
HE'S THE SONG,
HE'S THE SONG
IN THE DANCING OF THE SEA.

HE'S THE SONG,
HE'S THE SONG,
HE'S THE SONG
WHO COMPOSES ME.

HE'S THE SONG,
HE'S THE SONG,
HE'S THE SONG
IN THE DANCING OF THE SEA.

HE'S THE SONG,
HE'S THE SONG,
HE'S THE SONG
WHO COMPOSES ME.

The wind and waves pick up to normal speed again, rocking the ship to and fro as it did before the song. But NICHOLAS, the YOUNG SHIPMATE, and the SHIP'S CAPTAIN hold on tight to the mast, unmoved, as they are steadied by God's peace.

FADE TO BLACK.

ACT 3, SCENE 5 - THE SPIRIT

The same ship, the same scene, with NICHOLAS, the SHIP'S CAPTAIN, and the YOUNG SHIPMATE still holding on to the mast. The storm continues but is somewhat calmer.

NICHOLAS

(to the YOUNG SHIPMATE)

You remind me of someone I left back on shore. Him and his two friends.

YOUNG SHIPMATE

Why do I remind you of him? Was he as scared as I am right now?

NICHOLAS

(laughing)

No. But thinking about some of our adventures, it gives me hope that we might survive this one, too.

SHIP'S CAPTAIN

What happened? We could all use some hope right now.

NICHOLAS

I remember telling them stories about all the miracles God performed with the weather: when Jesus calmed the storm by speaking to it, when Moses split the Red Sea by raising his staff in the air, and when Joshua and his priests stopped a river from flowing as soon as they stepped into it.

YOUNG SHIPMATE

How did they do it?

NICHOLAS

We never figured it out! We tried doing some of those things ourselves at times, holding our hands in the air to stop the rain, but it just poured harder! Or stepping out of a boat to walk on the water, but we sank right down as always. We thought we didn't have enough faith or strength or whatever it takes.

YOUNG SHIPMATE
Do you think you know what you did wrong?

NICHOLAS
Well, it wasn't that we did anything wrong, exactly. It was just that God had a reason for each of those miracles to occur. God doesn't do miracles on a whim, just for our entertainment. He does them because He has places for us to go, things He wants us to do, people He wants us to see. And sometimes doing those things just isn't possible without some kind of miracle.

YOUNG SHIPMATE
You mean, they were desperate, like we are? And *that* gives you hope?

NICHOLAS
Not just desperate, but desperate for God to do something miraculous. It was like they knew what God wanted them to do, so they reached out to Him in faith. And when they did, their steps of faith and God's will caused the miracle to happen.

SHIP'S CAPTAIN
So if God wants a miracle to happen, why doesn't He just do it Himself?

NICHOLAS
I'm still working that one out. But it's as if it's not enough just for God to want it to happen. He's looking for people here on earth who want it to happen, too. Then, when His will and our will connect, the miracle bursts forth! Whether it was Moses lifting his staff or Peter stepping out of the boat or the priests stepping into the river, God's will intersected with their steps of faith, and that's what ignited the miracle.

SHIP'S CAPTAIN
So what do we do?

NICHOLAS
Standing orders are good orders, right? If God wants us to get to the other side in a hurry, maybe the storm isn't *against* us! Maybe it's for

us! Maybe the storm's actually the *answer* to our prayers! We just need to pray that God will use it to get us where we need to go, right when He wants us to get there.

SHIP'S CAPTAIN

If that's true, we've got to step out in faith now. There's no time to lose!

NICHOLAS

No time at all!

SHIP'S CAPTAIN

(blowing a whistle and calling out)

Crew! Gather 'round! We're going to pray! Nicholas?

NICHOLAS

Crew! The God whom I serve and who Has given us our lives wants us to reach our destination even more than we want to reach it! But we have to agree with Him in faith, here and now, that He not only *can* do it, but that He *wants* to do it. He's just waiting for us to step out in faith. If you love God, or even if you might want to love God, pray with me that we will reach our destination... and that the waves won't stand in our way!

As they pray, the unthinkable happens. The wind doesn't stop. It picks up speed, blowing more furiously than before. But as it does, the waves stop pelting the ship from every side. Instead, the wind, the waves, and the ship all head in the same direction, holding the ship on a steady and impressively fast course. The men are amazed by the speed. Some run to the sides to look ahead, some hold their hands up to heaven, feeling the rain, and some look at each other in amazement. Unseen by the CREW MATES, a figure appears, THE HOLY SPIRIT, at the front of the boat, taking hold of the waves (in the form of long, wide ribbons of flowing fabric) and allowing the ship to move steadily forward.

SHIP'S CAPTAIN

It's as if an invisible hand is holding the rudder! But that's impossible. We let go of the rudder long ago when the winds reached gale force.

NICHOLAS
Impossible! Or a miracle.

YOUNG SHIPMATE
Or both!

SHIP'S CAPTAIN
Storm or no storm, we've got to go home.

NICHOLAS
And *because* of the storm, we might actually make it there on time.

The music swells with a reprise of the chorus from "Storm Or No Storm," sung by all on board.

12. STORM OR NO STORM (REPRISE)

CREW MATES
STORM OR NO STORM,
THE SPIRIT SAYS GO,
SO LET IT BLOW!

STORM OR NO STORM,
MY SPIRIT SAYS GO,
SO LET IT BLOW!

OH, O-OH, O-O-OH!

As the ship picks up speed, the CREW MATES whoop and holler, waving their hats (for those who still have them) and cheering on the storm in the direction that it's blowing. As the music reaches its climax, the lights FADE TO BLACK.

ACT 3, SCENE 6 - THE GRAIN

Day breaks off the coast of Myra, which is visible on the horizon beyond the ship. During the dialog below, the ship moves toward Myra and a dock comes into view. NICHOLAS, the SHIP'S CAPTAIN, and the YOUNG SHIPMATE can be seen with the other CREW MATES onboard, looking in awe at the sight.

YOUNG SHIPMATE
I can't believe it! Land!

SHIP'S CAPTAIN
Land is right!

NICHOLAS
And not just any land... it's Myra! I'd recognize it anywhere. That's not far from where I departed when I came to the Holy Land! Somehow God really has brought me... home!

The CREW MATES look in awe, too, cheering that they've survived their ordeal at sea.

SHIP'S CAPTAIN
Five days to Myra?!? That's impossible. It would have taken us weeks to get this far if we had gone around the sea as I had planned. And even if we had tried to go straight across, we would never have made it this fast without that strong wind. That wind must have been the breath of God!

NICHOLAS
Those people running up to the dock... what are they saying?

SHIPMATE #1
Something about "an answer to our prayers"...

SHIPMATE #2
"The famine," that's what I heard...

SHIPMATE #1
With all that water we just came through, they're talking about a famine?

SHIP'S CAPTAIN

The famine has affected the whole northern coast. These storms we just came through must not be making it to shore.

The dock appears onstage with the ship beside it now. The residents of Myra are streaming up to see the ship.

VARIOUS RESIDENTS OF MYRA

"It is a miracle!"
"God has provided!"
"A whole ship, filled with grain!"

NICHOLAS

They seem to think we're an answer to their prayers!

SHIP'S CAPTAIN

(looking bewildered)

I wish we were. But how can we be?

NICHOLAS

You said yourself the drought has reached here. I'm sure this ship looks to them like a field of grain sprouting in a desert.

SHIP'S CAPTAIN

But this grain's got to get to Rome. Every piece of it. The ship was carefully weighed in Alexandria before we left, and it has to be the exact same weight when we reach Rome or I'll be held responsible. Me and all my crew.

YOUNG SHIPMATE

After what we just came through... don't you think all this grain would have been at the bottom of the sea by now if Someone hadn't been watching over us?

SHIP'S CAPTAIN

It *is* a miracle. Five days to Myra. Just five days. And yet...

NICHOLAS

And yet?

SHIP'S CAPTAIN

And yet, there's still a drought in Rome, too.

NICHOLAS

(thinking)

That's true. How can we know if God wants this grain to go to this city or to another? Or perhaps to both?

SHIP'S CAPTAIN

I don't know how it could go to both unless God multiplies it. Wasn't there a story like that about Jesus?

NICHOLAS

Yes, He was a master at multiplication.

VARIOUS RESIDENTS OF MYRA

(now taking hold of the ropes that are being thrown from the ship)

"It's a miracle!"
"There's no better time!"
"God has answered us from heaven!"

YOUNG SHIPMATE

(looking at the SHIP'S CAPTAIN)

What are you going to do?

SHIP'S CAPTAIN

Just what Nicholas and I agreed last night in the middle of the storm. We said if we ever made it to shore, the first thing we were going to do...

NICHOLAS

...was to go to the nearest church and give thanks to God. (then with a sudden realization) And I know just where that church is. (to the SHIP'S CAPTAIN) Secure the boat! (to the YOUNG SHIPMATE) Round up the crew! I'll speak to the people. I know just where we'll go.

The music swells with a reprise of "He's The Song," sung by all the CREW MATES as they secure the ship to disembark.

13. HE'S THE SONG (REPRISE)

CREW MATES

HE'S THE SONG,
HE'S THE SONG,

HE'S THE SONG
IN THE DANCING OF THE SEA.

HE'S THE SONG,
HE'S THE SONG,
HE'S THE SONG
WHO COMPOSES ME.

As the song ends, NICHOLAS and the SHIP'S CAPTAIN lead the rest of the CREW MATES to shore, some of them hugging the people, others bending down to kiss the ground, as the lights FADE TO BLACK.

END OF ACT 3

ACT 4, SCENE 1 - THE DREAM

A group of priests gather around one of their own, PRIEST #3, who sits on a stool in the center of a church in Myra. The other PRIESTS are listening to his story with rapt attention when suddenly they break into song with words of astonishment. This is a lighthearted scene, comedic in effect because of their surprise, but not slapstick. Dimitri introduces the scene.

DIMITRI

Meanwhile, back in Myra, a different kind of storm had been brewing. The old bishop of Myra has died, and for three days the priests have been puzzling what to do. But the night before the boat arrives, one of them has a dream.

14. HIS NAME WAS NICHOLAS

PRIEST #1

(spoken with a huff)

NICHOLAS?!?

PRIEST #2

(spoken with sarcasm)

NICHOLAS?!?

PRIEST #3

(spoken with affirmation)

NICHOLAS!!!

PRIEST #1

THERE'S NO ONE IN THIS TOWN NAMED NICHOLAS.
NEVER EVEN HEARD THAT NAME.

PRIEST #2

THERE'S NO SUCH MAN, IT SEEMS RIDICULOUS.
JUST A DREAM, STILL ALL THE SAME?

PRIEST #1

YOU SAY YOU HAD A DREAM LAST NIGHT,
AND OUT OF HEAVEN CAME A LAD

PRIEST #2

TO TAKE OUR PRECIOUS BISHOP'S PLACE,

GOD REST HIS SOUL, NOW THREE DAYS DE-AD?
(sung in barbershop style)

The music stops as they all bow their heads and make the sign of the cross.

PRIEST #3

(spoken)
THAT'S WHAT I SAID!
(sung)
HIS NAME WAS NICHOLAS.

PRIEST #1

MAYBE ICARUS?

PRIEST #3

CLEARLY NICHOLAS.

PRIEST #2

NOW DON'T TICKLE US!

PRIEST #3

NO I'M SERIOUS!
AND HE'S QUITE A MAN.
HIS NAME WAS NICHOLAS.

PRIEST #2

DON'T BE FRIVOLOUS!

PRIEST #3

I'M METICULOUS.

PRIEST #1

DREAMS CAN CRIPPLE US.

PRIEST #3

DREAMS DELIVER US
AS THEY OFTEN HAVE.

REMEMBER JOSEPH IN HIS CELL?
TWO DREAMS TO HIM, TWO MEN DID TELL.

PRIEST #1

BOTH DREAMS CAME TRUE
IN THREE DAYS TIME,

PRIEST #2

AND JOSEPH WAS
FREED FROM HIS CRIME.

PRIEST #1

AND THE OTHER JOSEPH, JUST AS TRUE,
HE HAD A DREAM ONE NIGHT LIKE YOU.

PRIEST #2

THE NAME OF JESUS CAME TO HIM
STRAIGHT FROM AN ANGEL, NOT A WHI-M.
(again in barbershop style)

PRIEST #3

(spoken)
AND YOU BELIEVE HIM?!?
(sung)
HIS NAME WAS NICHOLAS.

PRIEST #1

AND HE'LL VISIT US?

PRIEST #3

HE WILL VISIT US.

PRIEST #2

DOUBT THE LITTLEST?

PRIEST #3

GOD WILL GIVE TO US
SOMEONE FROM HIS HAND.
HIS NAME WAS NICHOLAS.

PRIEST #1

IT'S FELICITOUS!

PRIEST #3

IT'S JUST NICHOLAS.

PRIEST #2

AND HE'LL VISIT US?

PRIEST #3

HE WILL VISIT US
RIGHT HERE WHERE WE STAND.

PRIEST #1

PERHAPS WE'LL ASK GOD FOR A SIGN
TO MAKE IT CLEAR WHAT'S ON HIS MIND.

PRIEST #2

WE'LL ASK HIM TO BRING THROUGH THAT DOOR
THE BISHOP WE'VE BEEN LOOKING FOR.

PRIEST #1

THE ONE THAT GOD WILL GIVE TO US
WILL HAVE THE NAME OF NICHOLAS.

PRIEST #2

THAT WOULD BE UNDENIABLE
AND PROVE DREAMS ARE RELI-A-B-LE.
(sung as before)

PRIEST #3

(spoken)
DON'T HOLD ME LIABLE! BUT...
(sung)
HIS NAME WAS NICHOLAS!

PRIEST #1

(with a shrug)
NICHOLAS!!!

PRIEST #2

(with a nod)
NICHOLAS!!!

PRIEST #3

(with conviction)
NICHOLAS!!!

After the song ends (and the applause, if any, dies down), the door bursts open and the CREW MATES from the ship pour in to say their morning prayers. The startled PRIESTS greet the crew as they enter, with the SHIP'S CAPTAIN and NICHOLAS entering last.

SHIP'S CAPTAIN

Thank you for letting us come in to say our morning prayers.

PRIEST #1

We're glad you're here.

SHIP'S CAPTAIN

We're glad we're anywhere! But especially here. We've been through quite a storm.

The SHIP'S CAPTAIN walks forward, then looks back at NICHOLAS who is following behind him.

SHIP'S CAPTAIN (CONT'D)
And thanks be to Nicholas for having the brilliant idea to come here today.

The PRIESTS look up, shocked that God could have already answered their prayers. They stare in disbelief at the SHIP'S CAPTAIN and NICHOLAS who walk forward to take their places at the front of the church as the lights FADE TO BLACK.

ACT 4, SCENE 2 - THE PRAYER

The same setting inside the church. The PRIESTS are finishing up leading their morning prayers for the CREW MATES.

PRIEST #3

(concluding his prayer)

"...and for all these things we thank You, Father. Amen."

ALL

(not necessarily in unison)

Amen.

The CREW MATES disperse, truly grateful, exiting the same door through which they entered. The SHIP'S CAPTAIN and NICHOLAS find each other in the crowd.

SHIP'S CAPTAIN

As soon as our prayers began, I knew what to do about the grain. I'd like to give a portion of it to the people here as an offering to God. It could only have been God's hand that steadied our rudder and brought us here so quickly. I'd rather take my chances with Rome than with God who brought us through that storm.

NICHOLAS

Agreed.

SHIP'S CAPTAIN

But will it be enough for all these people?

NICHOLAS

Jesus fed 5,000 with just five loaves of bread and two fish. And you have much more than that.

SHIP'S CAPTAIN

How did He do it?

NICHOLAS

All I know is He looked up to heaven, gave thanks to God, and began passing out the food with His disciples. In the end, everyone ate and was satisfied, and they still had twelve baskets full left over.

SHIP'S CAPTAIN

Then that's what we'll do, too. We'll look up to heaven, give thanks to God, and start passing out the grain.

NICHOLAS and the SHIP'S CAPTAIN are the last to walk to the door. The PRIESTS have been conferring as well, and they approach NICHOLAS before he exits.

PRIEST #2

Nicholas, is it? Could we have a word?

FADE TO BLACK.

ACT 4, SCENE 3 - THE ANSWER

NICHOLAS and the PRIESTS are still in the church, finishing up their conversation. Everyone else has left.

NICHOLAS
Just like that, you say? In a dream?

PRIEST #3
Just like that.

PRIEST #2
We'll leave you to consider it, Nicholas. If God is in this, He'll make it clear to you.

The PRIESTS start walking across the room, but PRIEST #3 turns to NICHOLAS to give him one parting thought.

PRIEST #3
One more thing, Nicholas. If you want to do this, our offer is open. But only if you want to do it. Dreams can help us know God's will, but God still takes our will into consideration. He always gives us a choice, Nicholas. The Holy Spirit, He is... a gentleman.

The PRIESTS walk to the other side of the room, leaving NICHOLAS to talk to God alone. NICHOLAS begins singing as he ascends the stairs to the second floor of the church.

15. THIS DAY AT THE CROSSROADS

NICHOLAS
LORD, THIS IS NOT
WHAT I THOUGHT IT WOULD BE
WHEN YOU CALLED TO ME FROM
THE FAR SIDE OF THE SEA.
THOUGH I KNEW I SHOULD COME
WITHOUT FURTHER DELAY,
WAS IT TRULY FOR THIS...
MOMENTOUS DAY?

THE GRAIN I COULD SEE
HOW THEY NEEDED IT MORE,
BUT THEN YOU STILL HAD SOMETHING ELSE
WAITING IN STORE.
A BISHOP THOUGH, LORD,
AND AS YOUNG AS I AM,

TO LEAD NOT JUST ONE CHURCH,
BUT MORE IN THIS LAND?

PRIEST #3
(still on the first floor, astounded)
HIS NAME WAS NICHOLAS!

PRIEST #1
I AM SO IMPRESSED!

PRIEST #3
(confounded)
IT WAS NICHOLAS!

PRIEST #2
WE ARE HEAVEN BLESSED!

PRIEST #3
(still shocked)
HE WALKED THROUGH THAT DOOR,
AND I ALMOST CRIED.
(now giddy)
HIS NAME WAS NICHOLAS!

PRIEST #1
(talking to PRIEST #2 about PRIEST #3, who is swooning)
WE WILL BE JUST FINE.

PRIEST #3
IT WAS NICHOLAS!

PRIEST #2
(again to PRIEST #2 about PRIEST #3)
WE JUST NEED SOME TIME.

PRIEST #3
BUT NOW NICHOLAS,
WHAT WILL HE DECIDE?

NICHOLAS
BUT CAN I MAKE THE SACRIFICE?
A LOVING WIFE, A FAMILY?
WHAT IF THE LIFE I'VE DREAMED ABOUT
IS DIFFERENT FROM YOUR DREAMS FOR ME?

I WANT TO WANT WHAT YOU WANT, LORD!
I KNOW THAT YOU HAVE DREAMS GALORE!
PLEASE HELP ME, LORD, TO UNDERSTAND.

PLEASE HELP ME, LORD, I'M JUST A MA-N.
(singing deeply on the last word, barbershop style)

NICHOLAS gestures to his throat, wondering what happened to his voice. The PRIESTS look up, too, wondering if he's already becoming one of them!

The chimes ring out the hour. It's 9 a.m., the same time the Holy Spirit showed up on the day of Pentecost. As the chimes continue to ring out the time, NICHOLAS runs his hands over a cross made of construction wood that is laying against a wall. A gilded cross hangs nearby, but he doesn't seem to notice it, taken instead by this wooden one. A vase filled with colorful flowers, including one golden one, stands on a table near the wooden cross.

NICHOLAS knows what to do. He lifts the golden flower from the vase and kneels at the foot of the wooden cross, surrendering his life once more to God.

After the chimes hit 9, there is silence. NICHOLAS slowly rises and starts to sing. His answer has come.

NICHOLAS

THERE IS A WAY
THAT SEEMS RIGHT TO A MAN.
IN THE END, ALL THAT MATTERS
IS WHAT'S IN YOUR PLAN.

WHAT WE GIVE UP ON EARTH
UP IN HEAVEN IS FOUND,
THE BLESSING OF FAMILY
AND LOVE ALL AROUND.

MY ANSWER IS "YES, LORD,"
NO MATTER THE QUESTION.
TO YOU I POUR OUT ALL MY
LOVE AND AFFECTION.

SEAL THIS ON MY LIPS,
HELP ME NEVER TO WAVER.
THIS DAY AT THE CROSSROADS
I'LL FOREVER SAVOR.

Outside the window, a commotion catches NICHOLAS'S attention. It's the SHIP'S CAPTAIN and his CREW MATES on the front steps of the church, lifting their hands to heaven, giving thanks to God, and passing out the baskets full of grain. The music swells as NICHOLAS watches. The PRIESTS ascend to where NICHOLAS is standing. NICHOLAS nods "Yes" to the PRIESTS and shakes their hands. They offer him a regal robe and a golden scepter, which he kindly declines, taking up his own cloak and his father's wooden staff instead. NICHOLAS and the PRIESTS descend the stairs together as the CREW MATES pour into the church and begin to sing.

PRIESTS

HIS NAME WAS NICHOLAS!

CREW MATES

HERE'S TO NICHOLAS!

PRIESTS

IT WAS NICHOLAS!

CREW MATES

CHEERS FOR NICHOLAS!

PRIESTS

GOD HAS GIVEN US
SOMEONE FROM HIS HAND.

ALL

(except NICHOLAS)

HIS NAME WAS NICHOLAS!
HERE'S TO NICHOLAS!
IT WAS NICHOLAS!
CHEERS FOR NICHOLAS!

NICHOLAS

(spoken)

THANKS, BUT REALLY!

(sung)

I AM JUST A MAN!

ALL

(lifting NICHOLAS into the air)

HIS NAME WAS NICHOLAS!
NICHOLAS!!!
NICHOLAS!!!
NICHOLAS!!!

FADE TO BLACK.

INTERMISSION

ACT 4, SCENE 4 - THE FLOWERS

As NICHOLAS walks through the streets of Myra, he sees a girl about twelve years old, YOUNG ANNA MARIA, selling flowers she has made out of braided blades of grass. Nicholas stops to talk to her, sensing God is near as Moses felt when he turned aside to look at the burning bush. Dimitri introduces the scene under a spotlight.

DIMITRI

Nicholas didn't become another man when he became a bishop. He became a bishop because of the man he already was. As he had done before with his father, he continued to do now: walking and praying and asking God where he could be of most help. It was on one of those walks that he met young Anna Maria.

The lights come up on the rest of the stage.

NICHOLAS

What do you have there?

YOUNG ANNA MARIA

Flowers! Flowers I've made of blades of grass. I braid them together like this, see?

NICHOLAS

I see! May I hold it?

She hands him the flower. He studies it, seeing its beauty even in its disheveled state, just as he sees God's beauty in the one who made it... even in her disheveled state.

NICHOLAS (CONT'D)

It's beautiful. I'd like to buy it, if I may.

YOUNG ANNA MARIA

One uncia, please.

NICHOLAS hands her a small coin. He considers the flower... and the plight of the girl.

NICHOLAS
What will you do with the money you make from selling these flowers?

YOUNG ANNA MARIA
It's for my sister, Sophia. She wants to get married, but my father doesn't have enough money for a dowry to offer to someone to marry her. He lost his business, and then our mother died. It's all made him very sad, him and my sisters, Sophia and Cecilia. I want to make them happy again.

NICHOLAS believes her as he has met others like her. He wishes he could buy every flower she has ever made, but knows it will take more than a basket of flowers to save this girl's sister.

NICHOLAS
And if she doesn't have a dowry, what will become of her?

YOUNG ANNA MARIA
My father says she'll have to go away where she can make money on her own. But I don't want her to go away, and neither does she. She's found someone she loves.

NICHOLAS
I see. And your other sister, Cecilia?

YOUNG ANNA MARIA
If Sophia can't marry, neither can Cecilia, and she'll have to go away, too.

NICHOLAS
And you?

YOUNG ANNA MARIA
(bursting into tears)
I don't want to go away!

She takes hold of NICHOLAS tightly, thankful that someone has noticed her plight.

NICHOLAS
(as YOUNG ANNA MARIA recovers from her tears)
Can you tell me your name and the name of your father? I'll pray for you all very, very hard.

YOUNG ANNA MARIA

My name is Anna... Anna Maria. And my father's name is Migel.

NICHOLAS

Well, young Anna Maria. You have my prayers, you and your whole family. Keep doing what you can do to help them, and keep trusting God to do what you can't. And thank you for the beautiful flower. I'll put it in a special place so I'll remember to pray for you.

He places the flower inside his cloak, next to his heart, and walks on.

FADE TO BLACK.

ACT 4, SCENE 5 - THE LOVE

YOUNG ANNA MARIA'S sister, SOPHIA, is waiting and watching for someone in her backyard. It's a charming but unkempt yard as flowers and bushes have grown unchecked. SOPHIA'S heartthrob, CASSIUS, appears beyond the fence.

CASSIUS
(whispering)
Sophia!

SOPHIA
(whispering, too)
Cassius!

CASSIUS
I couldn't let you go without saying something. Sophia, I...

SOPHIA
No, Cassius. Don't say it. If you say it, my heart will break into a million pieces.

CASSIUS
I don't want it to break into a million pieces. But if I don't say it, *my* heart will burst!

SOPHIA
There's no other way, Cassius! At least I can't see one if there is. We've only got tonight left. Tomorrow I'll be gone. So please, don't say it!

CASSIUS
(he jumps the fence and clasps her hands)
I know you're afraid, Sophia. I'm afraid, too. I'm afraid of losing you.

SOPHIA
(SOPHIA melts in his arms)
You'll never lose me, Cassius. Even if we're miles and miles apart.

CASSIUS
We can't let fear guide us. The fear is real, but God is real, too. I can't let you go without

saying it again... (he takes one hand) and again... (he takes the other hand) and again...

He gets down on one knee, still holding her hands, and begins to sing.

16. SOPHIA!

CASSIUS

SOPHIA, I LOVE YOU WITH MY WHOLE HEART!
SOPHIA, I LOVE YOU WITH MY SOUL!
SOPHIA, I LOVE YOU WITH AN EVERLASTING LOVE!
SOPHIA, YOU'RE THE HALF WHO MAKES ME WHOLE!

I LOVE YOU MORE THAN YOU'LL BELIEVE!
I LOVE YOU MORE THAN YOU CAN POSSIBLY RECEIVE!
BUT STILL I'LL TRY TO TELL YOU WHY,
'CAUSE I'LL KEEP LOVING YOU LONG PAST THE DAY I DIE,
AND HERE'S WHY!

SOPHIA, I LOVE YOU WITH MY WHOLE HEART!
SOPHIA, I LOVE YOU WITH MY SOUL!
SOPHIA, I LOVE YOU WITH AN EVERLASTING LOVE!
SOPHIA, YOU'RE THE HALF WHO MAKES ME WHOLE!

I COULD LOOK AT YOU FOR HOURS AND NOT GET BORED!
DAY AFTER DAY I LOVE YOU MORE!
I CAN'T THINK OF YOU WITHOUT A BIT OF BLUSHING,
'CAUSE THE BLOOD IN MY HEART, IT JUST STARTS GUSHING!

SOPHIA, I LOVE YOU WITH MY WHOLE HEART!
SOPHIA, I LOVE YOU WITH MY SOUL!
SOPHIA, I LOVE YOU WITH AN EVERLASTING LOVE!
SOPHIA, YOU'RE THE HALF WHO MAKES ME WHOLE!
THE HALF WHO MAKES ME WHOLE!

FADE TO BLACK.

ACT 4, SCENE 6 - THE COINS

NICHOLAS retreats to a cave hidden in a hillside where he keeps the inheritance he received from his parents. His plan is to give an anonymous gift to YOUNG ANNA MARIA'S family in a way that does not further humiliate her father, Migel.

NICHOLAS

(speaking to God)

Oh, God! I knew You wanted me to talk to her for some reason. I pray You'll help me pull this off.

NICHOLAS finds the opening to the cave, lights a lamp, and steps inside.

NICHOLAS (CONT'D)

There it is, still safe and sound.

He counts out a handful of coins and fits them into a small bag. He holds the coins and prays.

NICHOLAS (CONT'D)

Father, thank You for this gift from You. Let it bless others, too. Keep me hidden so they won't know. I pray Anna Maria's father receives it well and, not knowing who the donor is, doesn't try to return it for the sake of his honor. In Jesus' name, Amen.

NICHOLAS retreats back to the entrance of the cave and puts out the lamp. The scene shifts to the outside of YOUNG ANNA MARIA'S house. It's late at night, and the family is getting ready for bed. NICHOLAS overhears them as he waits at the window for an opportune moment.

YOUNG ANNA MARIA

Let's sing before bed, Sophia!

SOPHIA

I can't sing tonight, Anna. My heart is too heavy.

YOUNG ANNA MARIA

We have to try. We have to keep up our hope. We can't give up now.

SOPHIA

Anna, you amaze me with your hope. And your flowers. And all you do for all of us. I'll sing. But you'll have to help me. You, too, Cecie.

CECILIA

I'll hum. You sing.

YOUNG ANNA MARIA

I'll hum, too. It's up to you, Sophie.

SOPHIA

(resigned, knowing it's pointless to argue)

You know I wouldn't do it if it was anyone else asking me.

YOUNG ANNA MARIA

(smiling)

I know.

SOPHIA begins to sing, reprising the song that CASSIUS sang to her earlier, but also applying the words to her sisters.

17. SOPHIA! (REPRISE)

SOPHIA

I LOVE YOU MORE THAN YOU'LL BELIEVE.
I LOVE YOU MORE THAN YOU CAN POSSIBLY RECEIVE.
BUT STILL I'LL TRY TO TELL YOU WHY,
'CAUSE I'LL KEEP LOVING YOU LONG PAST THE DAY I DIE...

She breaks down during the last line, and the music stops. CECILIA and YOUNG ANNA MARIA hold her tight. MIGEL comes in when he hears the crying.

MIGEL

You have such faith, Anna. And you, Sophia. Your voice is like an angel. I don't know how we'll make it through the days ahead.

He chokes back his emotion.

CECILIA

Father, can we pray one more time? Perhaps there's still a way. Please, Father?

MIGEL

Yes, Cecilia. We can never say too many prayers.

They all bow and begin to pray, inaudible to the audience.

NICHOLAS takes out his bag of coins and holds them up in prayer, smiling as he senses God is answering his own prayers, too... through him.

When the family finishes their prayers and says their goodnights, MIGEL leaves the room and puts out the light.

NICHOLAS stands and walks closer to the window, but a passerby approaches from the other direction. He continues walking until the coast is clear, then makes his way back to the window. He holds up the bag as if weighing the gold in his hands one more time, then tosses it up and into the open window in a graceful arc. The bag lands with a thud and a few coins roll out. NICHOLAS exits.

The house lights up again, and the girls pick up the bag. Some coins spill onto the floor. They're astounded. MIGEL enters the room.

MIGEL
I heard something!

CECILIA
(holding up the bag and picking up some coins from the floor)
It was this! And these!

MIGEL
What?!? How?!?

He runs to the window and looks in both directions, but sees no one.

YOUNG ANNA MARIA
It's a miracle, Father! An answer to our prayers!

SOPHIA
(sorting through the coins)
It's enough for a dowry, Father! Just enough, but it's enough!

MIGEL
(sitting down)
I think it's time to pray again. I don't know who, and I don't know how. But no matter who or how, it had to be God who answered our prayers.

The last line of "Sophia (Reprise)" swells in the background as the lights FADE TO BLACK.

ACT 4, SCENE 7 - THE NEWS

During the blackout, DIMITRI shares some news.

DIMITRI

One day, three generals from Rome came to visit Nicholas. They brought good news and bad. The good news was when the Ship's Captain arrived in Rome, not an ounce of grain was missing! "It's a miracle," the Captain said. And because of his delivery, he was promoted to admiral. The bad news was that a new emperor had taken the throne, Diocletian. He was demanding all citizens worship him as a god. If not, they would face… consequences. But for now, Nicholas kept doing all he could to help as many as he could.

ACT 4, SCENE 8 - THE CATCH

Six months later, YOUNG ANNA MARIA is selling her braided flowers again on the street. NICHOLAS sees her and walks over.

NICHOLAS
More flowers! I've kept the last one quite safe.

He pats his cloak over his heart.

YOUNG ANNA MARIA
And God answered your prayers!

NICHOLAS
I hear Sophia's married now!

YOUNG ANNA MARIA
She is! But now we're praying for Cecilia. So I'm doing what you said... I'm doing what I can do and trusting God to do what I can't.

NICHOLAS
You're a smart woman, Anna Maria. And I'd like another flower, please.

YOUNG ANNA MARIA
(she brightens and offers one to him)
It's one of my best.

NICHOLAS
(choosing carefully from his coins and giving her one)
And here's one of my best. Does Cecilia have someone special in mind?

YOUNG ANNA MARIA
No. But I believe there's someone out there just for her. Like the song says.

NICHOLAS
The song?

YOUNG ANNA MARIA
The song our mother sang to us since we were little. She said she sang it before she met our father.

NICHOLAS
I'd love to hear it.

YOUNG ANNA MARIA
I could sing it now?

NICHOLAS nods and takes a seat on a nearby bench. YOUNG ANNA MARIA takes another flower in her hand, looking at it as she begins to sing.

18. LIKE A MIRROR TO MY HEART!

YOUNG ANNA MARIA
I BELIEVE
THERE IS SOMEONE
JUST FOR ME,
THERE MUST BE SOMEONE,
THOUGH I CAN'T SEE,
I KNOW THAT SOMEDAY I'LL FIND LOVE.

I BELIEVE
THERE IS SOMEONE
JUST FOR ME,
THERE MUST BE SOMEONE,
MY DESTINY,
SENT DOWN FROM HEAVEN ABOVE.

AND I KNOW
THERE'S SOMEONE FOR ME,
EVEN IF WE'RE MILES APART,
REFLECTING WHO
I'M MEANT TO BE,
LIKE A MIRROR TO MY HEART.

She dances and sings to her flower.

OH, I BELIEVE,
OH, I BELIEVE,
OH, I BELIEVE
THERE IS SOMEONE.

OH, I BELIEVE,
OH, I BELIEVE,
OH, I BELIEVE
THERE IS SOMEONE

JUST FOR ME,
JUST FOR ME,

JUST FOR ME,
JUST FOR ME.

YOUNG ANNA MARIA continues dancing with her flower until the music ends. NICHOLAS claps as she makes a slight curtsy.

NICHOLAS
You always give your best, don't you?

NICHOLAS smiles and looks at the flower she sold him, then puts it inside his cloak.

NICHOLAS (CONT'D)
Keep doing what you can do for your sister. And keep trusting God to do what you can't.

The lights FADE TO BLACK then return again as the scene changes to YOUNG ANNA MARIA's back yard. It's nighttime as NICHOLAS approaches the window where he stood six months earlier, listening again as the family gets ready for bed and waiting for an opportune moment to give them another gift.

YOUNG ANNA MARIA
Let's sing mother's song again, Cecie!

CECILIA
(almost in tears)
Just because Sophia was spared doesn't mean I will be, Anna.

YOUNG ANNA MARIA
I'll hum. You sing.

CECILIA
I'll hum. You sing!

YOUNG ANNA MARIA
All right, we'll both hum. I already sang it today, anyway.

CECILIA
You did?

YOUNG ANNA MARIA
Yes, on the street. For Nicholas! He bought another one of my flowers. He bought one just before Sophie was saved, too.

CECILIA

Nicholas, you say?

The two begin to hum.

19. LIKE A MIRROR TO MY HEART! (REPRISE)

CECILIA & YOUNG ANNA MARIA

LA-DEE-DA, LA-DEE-DA-A-DA.
LA-DEE-DA, DA-DA-DEE-DA-A-DA.
LA-DA-DEE-DUM,
LA-DA-DEE-DA-DA-DEE-E-DUM.

CECILIA goes to the window, glances out, and sings the words while YOUNG ANNA MARIA continues to hum.

AND I KNOW THERE'S SOMEONE OUT THERE,
DA-DEE-DA, DEE-DA-DEE-DUM,
DA-DA-DEE-DUM, LA-DA-DEE-DUM,
LA-DEE-DUM, OH, LA-DEE-DUM...

NICHOLAS backs away when he hears her coming closer, shaking his head with a "No, no, no!" when she says "and I know there's someone out there." He doesn't want to be discovered. They finish the song with humming, and CECILIA walks away from the window.

CECILIA

Time for bed, Anna.

They put out the light, and all is quiet. NICHOLAS waits, then decides to take his chance. He takes out his bag of coins, just like before, and lobs it into the window. It thuds on the floor and some coins jingle out. The light comes on quickly, and NICHOLAS begins to run. CECILIA is at the window.

CECILIA

It's Nicholas!

MIGEL rushes out the door and catches him before he leaves the yard.

MIGEL

Cecie wondered if it might be you! She was right!

NICHOLAS stops trying to break free and resigns himself to being caught.

MIGEL (CONT'D)

I don't want to harm you. I just want to thank you! You've done so much for us I couldn't have expected such a gift again. But your generosity... it's opened my eyes to the pride in my heart, a pride that almost cost me *two* daughters now.

NICHOLAS

Yes, I delivered the gifts, but it was God who gave them to me to give to you.

MIGEL

(looking up and down at NICHOLAS'S humble clothes)

But how...?

NICHOLAS

It's not from the church, and it's not from my own hand, but from my father's who earned it fairly from the work of his. He was a businessman like you. If he were alive today, I'm sure he would have wanted you to have it. He, of all people, knew how difficult it was to run a business, just as you do. And he loved his family very much, just as I see you do, too.

NICHOLAS pauses to let his words sink in, then continues.

NICHOLAS (CONT'D)

But please, tell no one of this. It was truly God Himself who answered your prayers. I'm just a tool in His hands, doing whatever I can that I know He wants done. I prefer to do my giving in secret, not even letting my left hand know what my right hand is doing.

MIGEL

God prompts many to be generous, Nicholas. But not everyone responds like you.

NICHOLAS

(leaning close to MIGEL and whispering now)

Now that you know my secret, if you need help again when Anna Maria is older, let me know. If God allows, I'll be happy to help her, too.

ROMAN SOLDIER

There he is! Seize him!

THREE ROMAN SOLDIERS take hold of NICHOLAS.

MIGEL

He's not done anything wrong! He's not taking, he's giving!

ROMAN SOLDIER

I don't know what you're talking about. We have orders from Rome to arrest this man.

They lead NICHOLAS forcefully off the stage, leaving the TWO GIRLS and MIGEL stunned at yet another unexpected turn of events.

FADE TO BLACK.

END OF ACT 4

ACT 5, SCENE 1 - THE RIDE

NICHOLAS and the THREE PRIESTS are taken to a Roman prison by horse-drawn wagon, driven by a Roman soldier. They're shackled to the wagon, discussing the events of the night.

PRIEST #1
They've burned the church...

PRIEST #2
They've burned the Scriptures...

PRIEST #3
And they're arresting anyone who won't bow to Caesar and worship him like a god.

PRIEST #1
They gave us one last chance to worship Caesar, but we wouldn't, of course, so they put us in chains.

PRIEST #2
And that's when they went looking for you.

NICHOLAS
So it's happening, just as the generals warned.

PRIEST #3
This new Caesar, this Diocletian... a new name to be feared.

NICHOLAS
I don't fear Diocletian. But I do fear for those in our church. What will happen to them? Will they be able to maintain their faith... to the end? I pray God leads them better than we ever could.

PRIEST #1
It's not that we want to defy Rome. We want to honor those in authority, as Jesus taught.

PRIEST #2
But to deny that Jesus is our Lord is like denying that the sun rose this morning! I just couldn't do it.

NICHOLAS

Neither could I. How could I deny the One who gave me life and faith and hope in the darkest hours of my life? If denying Christ means I have to wear these chains, so be it. But to say a man like Diocletian is God, and that Jesus is not, that's unconscionable. Not that I look forward to what awaits us in prison.

PRIEST #3

(pausing as he considers what lies ahead)

I hear the isolation is the worst. But no matter what awaits us, Nicholas, know that we are with you in spirit.

NICHOLAS

And I with you, my brothers. The same God who's been with us until now will be with us to the end.

FADE TO BLACK.

ACT 5, SCENE 2 - THE SANCTUARY

NICHOLAS sits alone in his prison cell. The room is small and claustrophobic with barely enough room to stretch his full body in any direction. The side of his cell facing the audience has been removed so they can see him. The lighting is dark and somber.

NICHOLAS
(talking to himself as much as to God)
Tight spaces. You know I hate tight spaces.

He tries to stretch, but can't. We feel claustrophobic for him.

NICHOLAS (CONT'D)
I've been able to take most anything, Lord. The lack of food, no lack of beatings, the stripes on my back every time they ask me to bow to Caesar. But these tight spaces, Lord. It makes me feel like I'm all alone, like I can't breathe.

He pauses and tries to take a deep breath, trying not to lose his composure.

NICHOLAS (CONT'D)
But I'm not alone, am I, Lord? Even though there are no snowflakes from heaven in here to remind me. I just need to know... You're still with me.

20. MY SANCTUARY

NICHOLAS

ALL I WANT,
ALL I NEED,
IS TO BE WITH YOU
AND TO KNOW YOU'RE NEAR.

ALL I WANT,
ALL I NEED,
IS TO TALK WITH YOU
AND TO KNOW YOU'LL HEAR.

AND I KNOW
THERE'S A PLACE

I CAN GO
TO FEEL YOUR PRESENCE.

OH, LORD,
BRING ME THERE!
BRING ME HOME.

INTO YOUR SANCTUARY,
OH, LORD!
INTO THE PLACE THAT YOU
CALL YOUR HOME.

INTO YOUR SANCTUARY,
OH, LORD!
FOR I KNOW
WHEN I'M THERE
I'M NOT ALONE!

ALL I WANT,
ALL I NEED,
IS TO BE WITH YOU
AND TO KNOW YOU'RE NEAR.

ALL I WANT,
ALL I NEED,
IS TO TALK WITH YOU
AND TO KNOW YOU'LL HEAR.

AND I KNOW
THERE'S A PLACE
I CAN GO
TO FEEL YOUR PRESENCE.

OH, LORD,
BRING ME THERE!
BRING ME HOME.

THIS IS MY SANCTUARY,
OH, LORD!
THIS IS THE PLACE THAT I
CALL MY HOME.

THIS IS MY SANCTUARY,
OH, LORD!
FOR I KNOW
WHEN I'M HERE
I'M NOT ALONE!
I'M NOT ALONE!

ALL I WANT,
ALL I NEED,
IS TO BE
IN YOUR PRESENCE.

ALL I WANT,
ALL I NEED,
IS TO BE
IN YOUR PRESENCE.

NICHOLAS	VOICE OF GOD (off stage, in a duet with NICHOLAS)
ALL I WANT,	THIS IS MY SANCTUARY.
ALL I NEED,	THIS IS MY SANCTUARY.
IS TO BE	THIS IS MY SANCTUARY.
IN YOUR PRESENCE.	THIS IS MY HOME!
ALL I WANT,	THIS IS MY SANCTUARY.
ALL I NEED,	THIS IS MY SANCTUARY.
IS TO BE	THIS IS MY SANCTUARY.
IN YOUR PRESENCE.	THIS IS MY HOME!

NICHOLAS
(renewed)
THIS IS MY SANCTUARY.
THIS IS MY SANCTUARY.
THIS IS MY SANCTUARY.
THIS IS MY HOME!

FADE TO BLACK.

ACT 5, SCENE 3 - THE ANGEL

NICHOLAS is still alone in his cell. Five years have passed. We see him talking to God again.

NICHOLAS

Father, thank You for turning this cell into a sanctuary. I don't know how I could have lasted this long if You hadn't. Those days in the Holy Land were sweet because I felt so close to You. But there's a sweetness in here that surpasses even that.

Still, I miss my friends. I miss talking to someone with skin on. I only see the guards and that's either to give me food or give me a beating. I never know which when the door opens.

After a few beats, the door creaks open and a modest light shines in. NICHOLAS reacts and squints. Someone peers through the doorway.

DIMITRI

(whispering)

Nicholas? Is that you?

NICHOLAS

I know that voice. It can't be!

DIMITRI

It is! I'm here.

NICHOLAS

Dimitri?

DIMITRI

(to the audience, along with YOUNG DIMITRI at his side)

Ah, yes, it's me, Dimitri Alexander, just a little bit older. Okay, a lot older, especially since it only six years later. But I'm telling the story, so let's roll with it. I'm still just as good looking though, right?

NICHOLAS

But how...?

DIMITRI
(entering cell)
Only God, Nicholas.

NICHOLAS
Only God! You're an angel!

DIMITRI
(shaking both of NICHOLAS'S hands, warmly)
I'm not much of an angel, Nicholas. But I am here!

NICHOLAS
You are here. It's like God with skin on.

DIMITRI
(looking closely at NICHOLAS)
Nicholas.

NICHOLAS
(looking closely at DIMITRI)
Dimitri.

They both sit against the wall, looking forward and not at each other. They sit in silence for several more beats, breathing and grateful, with no words needed as they realize they're really together again.

NICHOLAS
How long have I been here?

DIMITRI
Five years, I'm guessing. It's been almost six since I said goodbye to you in the Holy Land.

NICHOLAS
Six years. It's so good to see you.

DIMITRI
And you. You have no idea how good it is to see you. I've been looking for you for three months. You haven't been easy to find. I've only recently gotten out of my own version of this cell. I came straight across the sea to try to find you. I had to know where you were, how you were doing... if you were still alive.

NICHOLAS
I'm still alive, Dimitri, still very much alive. Sometimes you don't realize that Jesus is all you need until Jesus is all you have.

DIMITRI
I said the same to Ruthie! He is all we need. Because He has everything we need.

DIMITRI (CONT'D)
(pulling out a flower and looking at it)
All things come from Him, don't they?

NICHOLAS
And you've come from Him today, too.

At the mention of RUTHIE, NICHOLAS asks:

NICHOLAS (CONT'D)
And Ruthie... and Sammy? How are our young bodyguards doing?

DIMITRI hesitates, then decides to start from the beginning.

DIMITRI
You'd be so proud of them, Nicholas. After you left, they continued guiding pilgrims to the holy places on their own. They wanted to share with others the same good news about Jesus they had learned from you. But we all had to stop when the Great Persecution came.

NICHOLAS
Is that what they're calling it?

DIMITRI
(nodding)
The three of us weren't as well known as you, so we weren't arrested as quickly. We used our freedom to help as many as we could, seeing to the needs of those in prison and those who were still in hiding. But eventually, we were caught, too. The same questions, the same threats, the same torture we had seen others go through. Sammy and I were strong enough to withstand it. But Ruthie... she was too frail.

A pause.

DIMITRI (CONT'D)
One day, after being treated particularly harshly, she returned to us and collapsed. She had obviously been crying, but somehow still had a sweet smile on her face and in her heart.

"How can you do it," I asked. "How can you possibly smile after all that?"

Ruthie said, "I feel like I've been walking with Jesus for so long now that even if I die, death won't really change that. I'll just keep walking and talking with Him forever."

Sammy and I couldn't help but smile back at her. Her body was giving out, though, and she knew it. We could tell she was moments away from passing from this life to the next.

"You can't go!" Sammy said. "I need you! And there's still work to do here!" But he knew she was slipping away. Desperate, he said, "If you die, I'll pray God brings you back to life."

"You could, Sammy," she said. "But God's already brought me back to life once before when Nicholas came and introduced us to Jesus, so I know He'll do it again. And when He does, I'll go to live with Him forever."

And with that, she passed through the veil and saw God face to face, walking and talking with Him as she had always done before.

NICHOLAS continues to sit in silence, thinking he should be sad, but feeling his heart soar again at Ruthie's faith instead.

NICHOLAS
Either way we win, don't we, Dimitri? Either we die and get to be with Jesus or we live and get to continue His work here. Either way we win.

DIMITRI
Yes, either way we win.

NICHOLAS
Some people say I have great faith. But great faith doesn't come to those who have no doubts. Great faith comes to those who've had their

faith stretched so far it has to grow or else it would break completely. I needed to hear that story today, Dimitri.

DIMITRI

I want to hear all about you, too, Nicholas. But there's one more thing I want to tell you first.

He pauses. After an uncomfortable silence, NICHOLAS responds.

NICHOLAS

Yes?

DIMITRI

I've met someone. She's beautiful inside and out... stunning... and she loves Jesus very much. Her name is Anna Maria.

FADE TO BLACK.

ACT 5, SCENE 4 - THE GIRL

NICHOLAS and DIMITRI are still in NICHOLAS'S cell, but during the blackout they've been hooked up to stage harnesses for what happens next.

DIMITRI

Yes, it's the same Anna Maria you know! When I was looking for you, I found her! She's almost eighteen now.

NICHOLAS

(smiling)

You'll have to tell me the whole story.

DIMITRI

I will. But I can't just tell it. I have to sing it!

A trill of music plays. The walls and ceiling of the cell fall to the floor, opening up NICHOLAS'S cell so NICHOLAS and DIMITRI are free to soar as the story unfolds.

DIMITRI helps NICHOLAS to his feet, and they are whisked up and away to the other side of the stage where we see the same street scene where NICHOLAS met YOUNG ANNA MARIA. Adult ANNA MARIA is there now, selling her braided flowers. DIMITRI describes what happened in a song.

21. CATCH ME! I'M FALLING IN LOVE!

DIMITRI

IN MY JOURNEY TO FIND
WHERE YOU MIGHT BE,
I MET ON MY WAY... ANNA MARIA.

"HAVE A FLOWER?" SHE SAID,
AND I NODDED MY HEAD,
THEN I FOUND WORDS AND SAID, "SO NICE TO MEET YA!"
"IS THERE SOMEONE NAMED NICHOLAS AROUND?"
AND SHE GASPED AND DROPPED TO THE GROUND!

THEN A STORY SHE TOLD
ABOUT TWO BAGS OF GOLD.
I GREW SUDDENLY BOLD
FOR A THIRD BAG TO HOLD
AS MY HEART HAD BEGUN TO UNFOLD.

DIMITRI and NICHOLAS soar across the stage to another set. On their way, they soar past a silvery moon. A tug on the rope makes NICHOLAS say "Ho-ho-ho!" as they pass in front of the moon, creating an iconic image of St. Nicholas. They land on the other side of the stage where NICHOLAS himself had once stood at the girls' window.

TO HER WINDOW I RAN,
WITH THE GOLD IN MY HAND
I HAD EARNED IN THAT MOST HOLY LAND.

SET THE BAG DOWN INSIDE,
THEN I RAN OFF TO HIDE,
PRAYING SOMEDAY WE'D SIT SIDE-BY-SIDE.

THEN I PRAYED THAT SOMEHOW I'D FIND YOU.
GOD GRANTED THAT PRAYER NUMBER TWO!

BACK TO PRAYER NUMBER ONE,
NOT TO SAY YOU'RE NOT FUN,
BUT SWEET ANNA MARIA,
SHE'S NATURALLY A
BRIGHT ANGEL FROM HEAVEN ABOVE!
CATCH ME! I'M FALLING IN LOVE!

LA-DEE-DA, LA-DEE-DA-DA!

NICHOLAS catches DIMITRI as they land back inside the prison cell. The walls and ceiling go back up and NICHOLAS and DIMITRI lean against the wall again as they had done before.

FADE TO BLACK.

ACT 5, SCENE 5 - THE RELEASE

Still inside NICHOLAS'S cell. Another five years have passed, and NICHOLAS is asleep on the floor. DIMITRI stands outside the door once again. The guard opens it for him this time.

DIMITRI
(putting his head through the doorway)
Nicholas! It's time to go. You're free!

NICHOLAS hardly stirs.

DIMITRI
I said, you're free! You can go home.

At the mention of the word "home," NICHOLAS perks up.

NICHOLAS
Home?

DIMITRI
(DIMITRI sits down next to NICHOLAS as the guard leaves, keeping the door open)
Yes, home! The emperor has issued a decree for all Christians to be released.

NICHOLAS
Diocletian is releasing us?

DIMITRI
No, there's a new emperor now. Constantine. So much has changed since I saw you here five years ago! Constantine has reversed Diocletian's decree and set all Christians free! Even Diocletian's wife and daughter have become Christians!

NICHOLAS looks at DIMITRI, impressed.

NICHOLAS
God does answer our prayers, even from in here.

DIMITRI
As much as Diocletian changed the world for bad, Constantine is changing it for good. One person really can affect the course of history, whether for bad or good.

It's just as you told us: each of us has just one life to live. But if we live it right, one life is all we need. You're free!

NICHOLAS

Oh, Dimitri, thank you for coming to get me. Of course, between talking to God and seeing you on your last visit, I've been free for a very long time. But I *would* like to go home.

As DIMITRI helps NICHOLAS to his feet, the cell breaks open again and is whisked off the stage. They walk across to the street scene where ANNA MARIA greets them. She's five years older, too, with two small children playing nearby.

ANNA MARIA

(running to him and holding him tight)

Nicholas!

NICHOLAS

Anna Maria!

ANNA MARIA'S CHILDREN

(running to DIMITRI and giving him a hug)

Daddy!

NICHOLAS looks at DIMITRI and DIMITRI shrugs. ANNA MARIA hands NICHOLAS his staff.

NICHOLAS

(looking at his staff with affection)

I was afraid I'd lost you. But I see you've been here all along.

He looks at the family and smiles again as the lights FADE TO BLACK.

END OF ACT 5

ACT 6, SCENE 1 - THE INVITATION

Twelve years have passed since NICHOLAS got out of prison. He's walking and talking along a country road with DIMITRI.

NICHOLAS
And you've still never told her, after all these years?

DIMITRI
She's never asked. And even if I told her, she wouldn't believe me. She's convinced you did it.

NICHOLAS
But how could I have dropped a bag of gold through her window when she knew I was in prison? I can't believe it!

DIMITRI
In a way, she's right. It was you who inspired me to give her that gift. While you were in prison, lots of people started giving gifts in your name. You really did inspire them!

NICHOLAS
Of course, it was Christ who inspired me.

DIMITRI
And it was Christ who inspired me.

NICHOLAS
As long as He gets the credit in the end, I'm very well satisfied.

Changing the subject, NICHOLAS takes out a letter.

NICHOLAS (CONT'D)
You're sure she won't mind you being away for three months? I can still find someone else to accompany me.

DIMITRI
She's completely and utterly happy for me to go. It's unbelievable, isn't it?

NICHOLAS
It's right here in black and white.

He starts reading the letter.

NICHOLAS (CONT'D)
"By invitation of His Majesty, Emperor Constantine, to Nicholas, Bishop of Myra. You are herewith invited to a council of bishops at my palace in Nicaea for the months of May through August in the year of our Lord 325. You will be joining over 300 other bishops of the Christian church. I will be in attendance and presiding over the ceremonies. You may bring one personal attendant of your choosing..." That's you.

DIMITRI
I'm glad you chose me. I am honored. The only invitation we would have gotten under Diocletian would have been to our own execution.

NICHOLAS
Nearly everything has changed, Dimitri. Now the only barrier remaining to someone putting their faith in Christ is their own will, which at times can still be a mighty high barrier.

DIMITRI
The freedoms we've gotten since Constantine issued the new edict... it's true tolerance. To worship freely, travel freely (he indicates the road on which they're walking). He's given back church property that was taken away under Diocletian. I hear he's planning to build churches in the Holy Land over the spots where Jesus was born and died and other holy places.

NICHOLAS
Constantine's mother is apparently in charge of that. I heard she took a trip to see the same holy places you showed me, and she's planning to build churches over each of them. I'm sorry I have very little left to give to the cause. Between helping others before I was put in prison and the raids on the caves after that, this staff is about all I have left.

DIMITRI

But there's always something you can give, isn't there? And giving your time is just as important.

NICHOLAS

It's a bigger sacrifice for you, though, giving up *your* time with Anna Maria and your family to accompany me.

DIMITRI

After what we've been through, it doesn't sound like much of a sacrifice... spending three months at Constantine's summer palace. We'll be just fine. What could go wrong?

FADE TO BLACK.

ACT 6, SCENE 2 - THE WONDER

NICHOLAS and DIMITRI enter Constantine's summer palace in Nicaea, walking into a grand room which has seating for all the participants on raised platforms lining the walls. CONSTANTINE sits on a throne at the center of the stage, near the back, with his entourage filling in the spaces on both sides of him. A CHILDREN'S CHOIR enters, singing a song, with a few of the children holding swinging censers on ropes. Smoke rises from the incense that burns inside the censers.

22. WISPS OF SMOKE

CHILDREN'S CHOIR

WISPS OF SMOKE,
A FRAGRANT OFFERING UNTO YOU.
RISING UP,
CREATING SOMETHING FRESH AND NEW.

A NEW TIME,
A NEW SEASON,
A NEW START,
A NEW REASON,
A NEW DAWN,
A NEW FREEDOM.

WISPS OF SMOKE,
A FRAGRANT OFFERING UNTO YOU.
RISING UP,
CREATING SOMETHING FRESH AND NEW.

NICHOLAS

I NEVER THOUGHT I'D SEE
WHAT LIES BEFORE ME IN PLAIN VIEW.
I WONDER, "COULD IT BE
A BREATH OF LIFE AS I ONCE KNEW?"

CHILDREN'S CHOIR & NICHOLAS

A NEW TIME,
A NEW SEASON,
A NEW START,
A NEW REASON,

A NEW DAWN,
A NEW FREEDOM.

CHILDREN'S CHOIR/NICHOLAS (DUET)

WISPS OF SMOKE,	NEVER THOUGHT
A FRAGRANT OFFERING UNTO YOU.	WHAT LIES BEFORE ME IN PLAIN VIEW.
RISING UP,	"COULD IT BE
CREATING SOMETHING FRESH AND NEW.	A BREATH OF LIFE AS I ONCE KNEW?"

ALL IN ROOM

A NEW TIME,
A NEW SEASON,
A NEW START,
A NEW REASON,
A NEW DAWN,
A NEW FREEDOM.

CHILDREN'S CHOIR

WISPS OF SMOKE,
A FRAGRANT OFFERING UNTO YOU.
RISING UP,
CREATING SOMETHING FRESH AND NEW.

As the song ends, CONSTANTINE speaks.

CONSTANTINE

Welcome, everyone, to Nicaea.

FADE TO BLACK.

ACT 6, SCENE 3 - THE DIVINITY

Three days later, NICHOLAS and DIMITRI are walking through a palace hallway once again on their way to the grand meeting room.

DIMITRI

It's been an interesting three days, hasn't it? Why do you think Constantine is so interested in this gathering? He seems to have a personal stake in it... beyond just supporting the churches.

NICHOLAS

I think he wants to unify the empire... at all levels. And... there are various factions within the church he'd like to bring together.

DIMITRI

Like today, I suppose? I hear Arius is speaking this morning. This should be interesting. You don't think he'll hold much sway, do you?

NICHOLAS

I don't see how he can. Maybe his kind of thinking flies in Alexandria, but not throughout the empire. Too many lives have been affected by the persecution to put much stock in Arius's ideas. But we'll see what he has to say. I hear he's a great orator, even if we may disagree with his words.

They arrive at the grand meeting room and take their seats along with the others who have gathered. CONSTANTINE enters and all rise. CONSTANTINE sits and all sit. The MASTER OF CEREMONIES announces the next speaker.

MASTER OF CEREMONIES

Next we hear from Arius of Alexandria... speaking on the divinity.

Arius takes the floor and states his position in song.

23. JUST A MAN

ARIUS

SOME SAY JESUS AND GOD, THEY ARE ONE,
BUT DIDN'T JESUS SAY HE WAS GOD'S SON?

SO HOW CAN HE BE IN ANY WAY BOTH?
AND THEN THERE'S THIS MATTER OF THE... HOLY GHOST.

NICHOLAS
(to DIMITRI)
FATHER, SON, AND THE HOLY GHOST,
NOW THAT'S ONE GREAT TRINITY.
THREE-IN-ONE, NOW LET'S CALL THIS DONE!
THEY ARE ALL DIVINITY.

ARIUS
HE WAS CERTAINLY SPECIAL, I'LL GRANT YOU THAT.
BUT NOTHING LIKE GOD. HE WAS JUST A MAN.
JUST A MAN, I SAY, LIKE YOU AND LIKE ME,
PERHAPS A FEW BARS SHORT OF DIVINITY.

NICHOLAS
(to himself)
JUST A MAN, YOU SAY?
JUST A MAN, YOU SAY?
JUST LIKE YOU AND LIKE ME?
PLEASE DON'T KID WITH ME.
YOU'RE JUST KIDDING ME.
HE'S A DEITY!

ARIUS
HE DID GREAT THINGS, BUT BY HIS FATHER'S HAND,
NOT BY ANYTHING HE HAD PLANNED.
HE WAS JUST A MAN, I SAY. JUST A GOOD, SECOND BEST.
TO SAY ANYTHING ELSE WOULD MAKE GOD SOMEHOW LESS.

NICHOLAS
(standing now and singing to himself and
the audience, unnoticed by others on stage)
SECOND BEST, YOU SAY?
SOMEHOW LESS, YOU SAY?
GOD, WHO WOULD EVER HAVE GUESSED?
MY FATHER AND MOTHER BOTH
LIVED AND DIED FOR HIM.
I AM NOT IMPRESSED.

I AM ALIVE BECAUSE JESUS DIED!
I AM ALIVE BECAUSE JESUS DIED!
(higher and louder and drawing the
attention of those on stage)
I AM ALIVE BECAUSE JESUS DIED!
I AM ALIVE BECAUSE JESUS DIED!

ARIUS

LOOK WHO'S TALKING. IT'S NICHOLAS, RIGHT?
I HEARD YOU WERE LIKELY TO PUT UP A FIGHT.
WELL, PUT 'EM UP NOW, COME ON AND JUMP IN THE RING.
I'LL DUKE IT OUT WITH ANYONE, AND I EVEN SING.

NICHOLAS

(to the others in the room)

WITH CONSTANTINE HERE, IT IS PROPER AND FITTING
THAT WE ALL STAY SILENT AND JUST KEEP ON SITTING.
BUT HOW CAN WE SIT HERE AND NOT SAY A WORD
WHEN HIS WORDS STREAM OUT, DEMEANING OUR LORD?

I DIDN'T SPEND THOSE TEN YEARS IN A JAIL
TO LISTEN TO THIS MAN TELL HIS PLEASANT TALE.
I'VE BEEN BEATEN, I'VE BEEN TORTURED, JUST LIKE THE REST,
FOR OUR ONE TRUE MESSIAH, OUR GOD IN THE FLESH.

ARIUS

(to the audience)

BUT WHAT WILL THE BISHOPS EVENTUALLY CONCLUDE?
THAT'S ALL THAT MATTERS AND NOT WHAT HE'S BREWED.
WHAT IF THE FLOCK IN THE CENTURIES AHEAD
STARTS FOLLOWING MY WORDS AND THINKING INSTEAD?

NICHOLAS

HE IS LOVE, HE IS LIFE, AND WHAT I LOVE THE MOST,
HE LIVES IN ME THROUGH THE HOLY GHOST.
HE IS TRULY THE LIVING VINE,
FULLY HUMAN AND FULLY DIVINE.

LIKE THOSE WHO KILLED JESUS THE FIRST TIME AROUND,
YOU'RE DOING IT AGAIN, RIGHT HERE AND RIGHT NOW.
IN THEIR ZEAL TO DEFEND GOD, THEY HAD IT ALL BACKWARDS.
THEY KILLED HIM INSTEAD, THOSE INCREDIBLE...

MASTER OF CEREMONIES

(holding up his hand to NICHOLAS, with a nod toward CONSTANTINE)

MEN, INDOOR VOICES.

ARIUS

(sarcastically)

SHOW US YOUR PROOF, YOUR EVIDENCE, SIR,
OF HIS ETERNAL PRESENCE, HIS DIVINE NATURE.
WHAT MAKES YOU THINK THAT YOU'RE SMARTER THAN ME?
SHOW US YOUR PROOF AND THEN LET IT BE.

NICHOLAS

IT WAS NOT ON A WHIM ON A CROSS HE WAS HUNG,
BUT FOR SAYING THAT “I AND THE FATHER ARE ONE.”
“I’M IN MY FATHER, AND HE IS IN ME.”
THAT’S WHAT HE SAID BEFORE DYING FOR ME.

THEY PUT HIM TO DEATH FOR SPEAKING THE TRUTH.
YET, HERE YOU STAND, ASKING FOR MORE PROOF?
WELL, MY EVIDENCE IS HERE, RIGHT WHERE I STAND.

(NICHOLAS rips the robes off his back, revealing his scars)

I DIDN’T GET THESE FOR “JUST A MAN.”

There’s total silence, then a musical beat starts up again, briefly. The music stops, and Arius speaks, smiling smugly.

ARIUS

WELL, THEN IT LOOKS, SIR,
LIKE YOU WERE MISTAKEN.
AS I WAS SAYING...

The music picks up again, but ominously, as ARIUS begins mouthing more words, inaudible to the audience, continuing his speech as if ignoring NICHOLAS will make him go away.

As the music builds, so does NICHOLAS’S anger. Then NICHOLAS does the unthinkable. With no thought except to silence this man in front of him, NICHOLAS clenches his fist, draws back his arm, and, on the final note of the song, punches ARIUS squarely in the face.

ARIUS falls to the floor.

MASTER OF CEREMONIES

(pointing to NICHOLAS)

Arrest that man! And take away his staff.

The guards rush in, chaos ensues, and the lights FADE TO BLACK.

ACT 6, SCENE 4 - THE FRIEND

NICHOLAS is in a corner room, still in Constantine's summer palace, but under house arrest. The door opens quietly, and DIMITRI slips in.

NICHOLAS
How did you get in here?

DIMITRI
(smiling)
I've learned a thing or two on the streets... and about finding you in hard-to-find places.

NICHOLAS
What have I done, Dimitri?

DIMITRI
What have you done?! What else could you have done?! If you hadn't done it, someone else would have... or should have. You should have seen the look on Constantine's face. I could swear he was smiling.

NICHOLAS
Smiling? You know what I did was punishable by death... to strike someone in the presence of the emperor!

DIMITRI
He didn't appear to be bothered in the least. I think you did everyone in that room a favor. Even Arius. Who knows what God would have done to him if he had continued his diatribe.

NICHOLAS
(truly grateful) Thank you, Dimitri. (then serious) But it's hard to see any good that could possibly come of this. I've gone over and over it in my mind, and in every scenario, it seems I've just made the gravest mistake of my life. It'll be a long three months waiting to find out what the council decides about Arius's ideas... and me. This "house arrest." Even though it's the most beautiful prison I've ever been in, here in the corner of the emperor's palace, I feel more oppressed in here than in

the filthiest prison I was ever in for my faith. At least there, I was suffering for following my Lord. Here, the blame is on me. And worse, I fear I may have just won sympathy for Arius and his position. The bishops are likely to listen to him even more after what I did to him. I can never take it back.

DIMITRI

Maybe God doesn't want you to take it back. Maybe God is pleased with your heart that you wanted to stand up for Him. Sure, the punch may have been a bit overboard. But even Peter sliced off a man's ear in his zeal to defend Jesus.

NICHOLAS

And Jesus told him to put away his sword, then healed the man's ear.

DIMITRI

And Jesus eventually asked Peter to take care of His followers after His death.

Both sit in silence briefly, NICHOLAS unconvinced, but DIMITRI seeing the good that could still come from it.

NICHOLAS

Thank you... for being my friend.

FADE TO BLACK.

ACT 6, SCENE 5 - THE RESOLUTION

Three months have passed and NICHOLAS is still under house arrest in the palace. The door bursts open. It's DIMITRI, having been let in by the guards.

DIMITRI

They did it!

DIMITRI gives NICHOLAS a huge hug.

DIMITRI (CONT'D)

They did it! It's done! The council voted, and they agreed with you! All but two of the 318 bishops have sided with you over Arius!

Relief sweeps over NICHOLAS'S body.

DIMITRI (CONT'D)

And furthermore, the council decided not to take any further action against you!

Another visitor appears at NICHOLAS'S door. It's CONSTANTINE. A fresh wave of fear overtakes NICHOLAS for what he did in the emperor's presence.

CONSTANTINE

Nicholas, I wanted to thank you personally for coming here to be my guest. I'm sure this wasn't what you had planned, and it wasn't my plan for you. But even though you weren't able to attend the rest of the proceedings, I assure you, your presence was felt throughout every meeting.

What you did that day in my presence spoke to me more about about true faith than anything else I saw in the days that followed. I'd like to hear more from you in the future, if you'd be willing to be my guest again. But next time it won't be in the farthest corner of my palace.

Furthermore, I've asked for and received permission from the council to reinstate you to your position as Bishop of Myra. I believe the One who called you to serve Him there in the first place would want you to continue doing everything you've been doing up till now.

As for me, let me just say I appreciate what you've done here more than you can possibly know. Whenever you're ready, you're free to go home.

On hearing the word "home," NICHOLAS lights up. He's ready to get back to his flock. CONSTANTINE exits.

NICHOLAS

God, You've set me free again... in more ways than one.

A bright light appears over the heads of the audience, and a song begins, sung as before in the voice of NICK'S MOTHER from offstage.

24. HEALING COMES FROM HEAVEN (REPRISE)

The light illumines the THE HOLY SPIRIT, suspended high on a wire at the back of the theater, holding NICHOLAS'S staff and descending slowly to the stage in gentle swirls and twirls of poise and perfection. Reaching the stage by the end of the song, THE HOLY SPIRIT hands the staff to NICHOLAS who looks at it with affection.

NICK'S MOTHER (OFFSTAGE)

HEALING COMES FROM HEAVEN,
OF THAT YOU CAN BE SURE,
WHETHER BLOOD THAT SLOWS WHILE BLEEDING
OR THE BONES THAT MEND AND GROW.

YES, HEALING COMES FROM HEAVEN,
OF THAT YOU CAN BE SURE.
WE HAVE JUST TO REACH TOWARD HEAVEN
AND THEN WATCH THE HEALING FLOW!

SOMETIMES IT COMES SO QUICK
WE HARDLY UNDERSTAND.
SOMETIMES IT TAKES SO LONG,
BUT THEN WE STAND.

AND WE CAN ALWAYS KNOW
THAT ONE DAY WE WILL
BE MADE WHOLE
WHEN HEAVEN COMES TO STAY.

FADE TO BLACK.

END OF ACT 6

EPILOGUE - THE DENOUEMENT

DIMITRI sits on the same stool on which he sat during the PROLOGUE, stage left, lit by a single spotlight. Stage right is now set by the sea in the same place where NICHOLAS sang, "Is There Room For Me?" That part of the stage remains dark, however, until DIMITRI mentions it in his conclusion.

DIMITRI

So now you know a little more about me... Dimitri Alexander... and my good friend, Nicholas. He went back to his home after the conclave ended, spending another 18 years doing what he had always done: serving God and those he loved with all his heart, soul, mind, and strength. I was with him just a few days ago at his favorite spot in the world... by the sea.

The lights come up on the sea. An aged NICHOLAS (65) stands on the shore, watching an aged ANNA MARIA (54) playing on the shore with her little granddaughter, LITTLE RUTHIE.

DIMITRI (CONT'D)

He said he wanted to come to the shore one last time. So Anna Maria and I came, along with one of our grandchildren, little Ruthie.

LITTLE RUTHIE can be seen running back and forth in the waves, as ANNA MARIA tries to keep up with her.

He said looking back over his life, he never knew if he had accomplished what he had wanted to do: to make a difference in the world. He had seen glimpses along the way, of course, in the lives of people like me and Sammy and Ruthie; Sophia, Cecilia, and Anna Maria.

Perhaps his love for children was born out of losing his own parents at a young age. "Don't waste your pain," he said. "Don't get bitter. Make the world better." Of course, he knew God could use anything for good if we entrust our lives to Him.

I was intrigued by his answer to a question Ruthie asked there on the beach, when she ran up to him without a care in the world.

LITTLE RUTHIE and NICHOLAS act out the scene as DIMITRI describes it.

DIMITRI (CONT'D)

Nicholas's eyes were closed with his hands raised toward heaven, feeling the breeze. Ruthie reached out, tugged at his clothes, and asked, "Nicholas, have you ever seen God?"

He opened his eyes and looked at her, then smiled at me and Anna Maria. He looked at the sunshine and waves and miles of shoreline that stretched in both directions. Turning back to Ruthie, he said, "Yes, Ruthie, I have see God. And the older I get, the more I see Him everywhere I look."

Ruthie smiled and gave Nicholas a hug, then ran off to play as quickly as she had run up.

That was the last time I saw him until this morning. He asked if he could spend a few days alone with the Lord he loved. He said he had one more journey to prepare for. Anna Maria and I knew, of course, what he meant.

We knew he was getting ready to go home, to his real home, the one Jesus said He was going to prepare for all of us who believe in Him.

Nicholas had been looking forward to this trip his whole life. Not that he wanted to shortchange a single moment on earth, for he knew God had things for him to do here, too. But as his life here was winding down, he said he was ready to go. He said he was looking forward to everything God had in store for him next. He sent word to us this morning to come see him.

I have no idea how history will remember Nicholas, if it will remember him at all. He was no emperor like Constantine, no tyrant like Diocletian, no orator like Arius. He was just a man trying to live out his faith as best as he knew how.

He may have wondered if his life made any difference. I know my answer. And now that you've heard his story, I'll let you decide for yourself. In the end, I suppose only God really knows how many lives have been touched by this remarkable man who gave God credit for everything good he had done.

What I do know is this: each of us has just one life to live. But if we live it right, as Nicholas did, one life is all we need.

After a meaningful pause, the opening number kicks off again at full tilt, with images of St. Nicholas and Santa Claus throughout the ages and brief snippets about this man who has become so beloved around the world. Some of the facts for these snippets are included at the end of this script entitled "What We Know."

At one point in the montage, we see a rotund Santa on a rooftop trying to fit into a chimney as a voiceover of NICHOLAS says:

NICHOLAS

Tight spaces. You know I hate tight spaces.

The closing medley also serves as the curtain call, in which the CAST comes out to take their bows when the montage ends. NICHOLAS is the last to enter when the song changes and the cast sings "His Name Was Nicholas."

25. ST. NICK'S THEME/HIS NAME WAS NICHOLAS (REPRISE)

ALL

HIS NAME WAS NICHOLAS!
HERE'S TO NICHOLAS!
IT WAS NICHOLAS!
CHEERS FOR NICHOLAS!
GOD HAS GIVEN US
SOMEONE FROM HIS HAND.

HIS NAME WAS NICHOLAS!
HERE'S TO NICHOLAS!
IT WAS NICHOLAS!
CHEERS FOR NICHOLAS!

NICHOLAS

(spoken)

THANKS, BUT REALLY!

(sung)

I AM JUST A MAN!

The CAST cheers and lifts NICHOLAS into the air as they sing the final refrain...

HIS NAME WAS NICHOLAS!
NICHOLAS!!!
NICHOLAS!!!
NICHOLAS!!!

FADE TO BLACK.

THE END

WHAT WE KNOW

Here's what we know about some of the real-life events upon which this work is based.

- Nicholas was born sometime between AD 260-280 in the city of Patara on the northern coast of the Mediterranean Sea, a city you can still visit today in modern-day Turkey.

- Nicholas's parents were devout Christians who died in a plague when Nicholas was young, leaving him with a sizable inheritance.

- Nicholas made a pilgrimage to the Holy Land and lived there for a number of years before returning to his homeland.

- Nicholas traveled across the Mediterranean Sea in a ship that was caught in a storm. His ship miraculously reached its destination as if someone was holding the rudder, also called a tiller. Sailors on the Mediterranean Sea today still wish each other good luck by saying, "May Nicholas hold the tiller!"

- When Nicholas returned from the Holy Land, he took up residence in the city of Myra, about 30 miles from his hometown of Patara. Nicholas became the youngest Bishop of Myra and ministered there for the rest of his life.

- Nicholas secretly gave three gifts of gold, on three separate occasions, to a man whose daughters were to be sold into slavery because he had no money to offer to potential husbands as a dowry. In our version of the story, we've added the twist of having Nicholas deliver the first two gifts and Dimitri deliver the third to capture the idea that many gifts were given back then, and are still given today, in the name of Saint Nicholas, who was known for such deeds. This theme of redemption is also so closely associated with this story from Saint Nicholas's life that if you pass by a pawn shop today, you will often see three golden balls in their logo, representing the three bags of gold that Nicholas gave to redeem these three girls from their unfortunate fate.

- Nicholas pled for the lives of three innocent men who were unjustly condemned to death by a magistrate in Myra, taking the sword directly from the executioner's hand.

- "Nicholas, Bishop of Myra" is listed on some, but not all, of the historical documents recording those who attended the Council of Nicaea, which was convened by Emperor Constantine in AD 325. One of the council's main decisions addressed the divinity of Christ, resulting in the writing of the Nicene Creed, a creed which is still recited in many Christian churches today. Some historians say Nicholas's name does not appear on all the record books of this council because of his banishment from the proceedings after striking Arius for denying that Jesus was divine. Nicholas is, however, listed on at least five of these ancient record books, including the earliest known Greek manuscript of the event.

- The Nicene Creed was adopted at the Council of Nicaea and has become one of the most widely used, brief statements of the Christian faith. The original version reads, in part, as translated from the Greek, "We believe in one God, the Father Almighty, Maker of all things visible and invisible. And in one Lord Jesus Christ, the Son of God, begotten of the Father, the only-begotten; that is, of the essence of the Father, God of God, Light of Light, very God of very God, begotten, not made, being of one substance with the Father; By whom all things were made both in heaven and on earth; Who for us men, and for our salvation, came down and was incarnate and was made man; He suffered, and the third day He rose again, ascended into heaven; From thence he shall come to judge the quick and the dead..."

- Nicholas is recorded as having done much for the people of Myra, including securing grain from a ship traveling from Alexandria to Rome, saving the people from a famine.

- Constantine's mother, Helen, did visit the Holy Land and encouraged Constantine to build churches over the sites she felt were most important to the Christian faith. Two of those churches, The Church of the Nativity in Bethlehem and the Church of the Holy Sepulchre in Jerusalem, have been destroyed and rebuilt many times over the years, but are still in the same locations that Constantine's mother, and likely Nicholas himself, had seen.

- Nicholas died on December 6th, 343. You can still visit his tomb in the modern city of Demre, Turkey, formerly known as Myra, in the province of Lycia. Nicholas's bones were removed from the tomb in AD 1087 by men from Italy who feared they might be destroyed or stolen during an invasion by others. The bones of Saint Nicholas were taken to the city of Bari, Italy, where they are still entombed today.

- Of the many other stories told about or attributed to Nicholas, it's hard to know with certainty which ones actually took place and which were simply attributed to him because of his already good and popular name. For instance, in the 12th century, stories began to surface of how Nicholas had brought three children back to life who had been brutally murdered. Even though the first recorded accounts of this story didn't appear until more than 800 years after Nicholas's death, this story is one of the most frequently depicted in religious artwork associated with Saint Nicholas, featuring three young children standing next to Nicholas who had been raised to life. We have included the essence of this story in the form of the three orphans Nicholas met in the Holy Land and whom he helped to bring back to life spiritually.

Full Score
For Piano & Vocals

To listen to song samples
& orchestrations, visit:
HisNameWasNicholas.com

cue:
DIMITRI:
"His name was Nicholas...
and this is his story."

1. St. Nick's Theme

from His Name Was Nicholas

Eric Elder

B♭/E♭ A♭/E♭ E♭ A♭/E♭ B♭/E♭ A♭/E♭ E♭
Cm B♭
A♭ E♭/G Fm E♭ D♭
A♭/C B♭ B♭ B♭/D B♭/F
E♭/G A♭ B♭ E♭ A♭/E♭ E♭ A♭/E♭ E♭ A♭/E♭ E♭ A♭/E♭ E♭ A♭/E♭ E♭ A♭/E♭ E♭ A♭/E♭ E♭ A♭/E♭
rit.
accel.
E♭ A♭/E♭ E♭ A♭/E♭ E♭ A♭/E♭ E♭ A♭/E♭ E♭ E♭maj7
rit.

cue:
YOUNG NICK:
"Ready?!? Who wouldn't want to go on a treasure hunt?"

2. Who's It Going To Be Today?

from His Name Was Nicholas

Eric Elder

D♭
YOUNG NICK:
Who's it going to be to - day, Fa - ther? Who's it going to be to - day?
D♭
NICK'S FATHER:
Who's it going to be to - day, Fa - ther? Who's it going to be to - day? E - ven
D♭
B♭m
though we don't know, we will know when He shows us. So we'll go, then we'll know, yes, we'll
G♭maj7
YOUNG NICK:
know when He shows us! E - ven though we don't know, you will know, yes, you'll know. E - ven

A♭6
D♭
TOGETHER:
31
though we don't know, we will know?
Who's it going to be to - day, Fa - ther?
35
D♭
D♭
Who's it going to be to - day?
Who's it going to be to - day, Fa - ther?
39
D♭
D♭
Who's it going to be to - day?
We won't know till we know, but we'll know when He shows us. E - ven
43
B♭m
G♭maj7
though we don't know, we will go, and He'll show us. So we'll go, then we'll know, yes, we'll know, when He shows us! E - ven

A♭6
D♭/B♭
YOUNG NICK:
A♭
though we don't know, we will go!!! Who will it be? Tell me
G♭
E♭
NICK'S FATHER:
G♭m
A♭
(pause here as Nick places an orange, then returns)
who will we see? Keep your eyes o-pen wide, and you will see...
A♭
D♭
TOGETHER:
D♭
15ma
Who's it going to be to-day, Fa-ther? Who's it going to be to-day?
D♭
D♭
Who's it going to be to-day, Fa-ther? Who's it going to be to-day?

D♭
65
Who's it going to be to - day?
D♭
rit.
Who's it going to be to - day?
D♭
65

cue:
NICK'S MOTHER:
"Yes, healing comes from heaven, of that you can be sure..."

3. Healing Comes From Heaven

from His Name Was Nicholas

Eric Elder

Eb F Bb Eb
14
Some-times it takes so long, but then we stand! And we can al-ways know that
Db/Bb Db/Ab Dbsus/Gb Bb Eb
NICK'S FATHER
17
one day we will be made whole when heav-en comes to stay.
Heal-ing comes from heav-en, of
Db Eb Fm Bb
21
that you can be sure. E-ven fa-thers, moth-ers, doc-tors know that God's the One who cures. Yes,
Eb Db Eb
24
heal-ing comes from heav-en, of that you can be sure, so we pray to God in heav-en now to

D♭/B♭ B♭ E♭ YOUNG NICK: D♭/B♭ E♭
27
touch us here on earth! Some-times it comes so quick, we hard-ly un-der-stand.
E♭ NICK'S FATHER: F B♭ E♭ ALL TOGETHER: D♭/B♭ D♭/A♭
30
Some-times it takes so long, but then we stand! And we can al-ways know that one day we will be made whole when
a tempo
D♭sus/G♭ B♭ rit. E♭ YOUNG NICK: NICK'S FATHER:
34
heav-en comes to stay. Heal-ing comes from heav-en... Yes,
E♭/D♭ NICK'S MOTHER: A♭maj 7/C A♭mM7/B rit. E♭
37
heal-ing comes from heav-en... Please send a bit of heav-en our way.

cue:
NICK'S FATHER:
"...in His way,
in His time."
YOUNG NICK
enters the room...

4. Who's It Going To Be Today? (Minor)

from His Name Was Nicholas

Eric Elder

♩ = 100

C♯m C♯m

Piano

5

C♯m C♯m

YOUNG NICK:

Who's it going to be to - day, Fa - ther? Who's it going to be to - day?

9

C♯m/A C♯m/A

NICK'S FATHER:

Who's it going to be to - day, Fa - ther? Who's it going to be to - day? We won't

13

C♯m C♯m

know till we know, but we'll know when He shows us. E - ven though we don't know, we will go, and He'll show us.

C♯m
NICK'S MOTHER:
C♯m
Who's it going to be to-day, Fa-ther? Who's it going to be to-day?
C♯m/A
C♯m/A
NICK'S FATHER:
Who's it going to be to-day, Fa-ther? Who's it going to be to-day? E-ven
C♯m
A maj
though we don't know, we will know when He shows us. So we'll go, then we'll know, yes, we'll know, when He shows us. E-ven
F♯m7
YOUNG NICK:
C♯m
ALL TOWNSPEOPLE:
C♯m
though we don't know, we will know, yes, we'll know. We will know...? Who's it going to be to-

C♯m
C♯m/A
day, Fa-ther? Who's it going to be to-day? Who's it going to be to-
C♯m/A
C♯m
day, Fa-ther? Who's it going to be to-day? We won't know till we know, but we'll
A maj
F♯m7
know when He shows us. E-ven though we don't know, we will go, and He'll show us. So we'll go, then we'll know, yes, we'll
espress.
C♯m
C♯m/A
G♯m7
A maj/F♯
YOUNG NICK:
know, when He shows us. We will go. Who will it be? Tell me who will we

F♯m/D
F♯m6/D
E♭
50
NICK'S FATHER:
rit.
rit.
see? Keep your eyes o-pen wide, and you will see...
54
♩ = 92
NICK'S MOTHER:
E♭ D♭ E♭ Fm B♭
Heal-ing comes from heav-en, of that you can be sure, wheth-er blood that slows while bleed-ing or the bones that mend and grow. Yes,
58
E♭ D♭ E♭ D♭/B♭ B♭
heal-ing comes from heav-en, of that you can be sure. We have just to reach toward heav-en and then watch the heal-ing flow!
62
E♭ D♭/B♭ E♭ E♭ F B♭
Some-times it comes so quick, we hard-ly un-der-stand. Some-times it takes so long, but then we stand!

4. Who's It Going To Be Today? (Minor)

cue:
YOUNG NICK:
"Oh, I know You'll be with me here. I just wish I could be with You there."

5. Is There Room For Me?

from His Name Was Nicholas

Music by Eric Elder
Lyrics by Annette Carden-Dale

B♭ E♭ A♭/E♭
where You are? I won't
B♭/E♭ A♭/E♭ E♭ A♭/E♭ B♭/E♭ A♭/E♭ E♭ A♭/E♭ B♭/E♭ A♭/E♭
be long in this place, and I don't take up too much space. I just want to see Your
E♭ A♭/E♭ B♭/E♭ A♭/E♭ E♭
face and rest in - side Your warm em - brace. Do You re -
Cm B♭
mem-ber me? Do You re - mem-ber me? Do

Ab
Eb/G
Fm
Eb
Db
You re - mem - ber me, Dear Lord, where you are?
Ab/C
Bb
Bb
Bb/D
Bb/F
rit.
Eb/G
Ab
Bb
Eb
Ab/Eb
Eb
Ab/Eb
Eb
accel.
Ab/Eb
Eb
Ab/Eb
Eb
Ab/Eb
Eb
rit.
Ab/Eb
Eb
Ebmaj7

cue:
NICHOLAS:
"But I think I've just seen the first one... right here."

6. Here I Stand

from His Name Was Nicholas

Eric Elder

Dsus
D5
Dsus
E
not where this place is. It's the touch of Your hand, it's the looks on their fa-ces. I did-n't know how I should
Esus
E5
Esus
F
an-swer the quest-ion, if I was or was not tru-ly deep down a Chris-tian. Yet You knew what I need-ed right
Fsus
F5
Fsus
G
now was a guide, for the mon-ey I've got, but a map I do not. Then I looked at his smile, with his

Gsus
G5
Gsus
A
Asus
32
hand o-pened wide, and I said in my heart, "Yes! The Lord will pro-vide!" So here I
Dsus/A
A
Asus
G/A
A
37
stand in this Ho - ly Land, stand-ing hand
Asus
Dsus/A
A
Asus
G/A
44
in hand with the Great "I AM!"

D
Dsus
D5
Now they say they will show me the most ho - ly plac - es. What I could-n't i - ma - gine and
Dsus
E
Esus
E5
now can't e - rase is the most ho - ly plac - es are those where Your grace is, where heav - en and earth are no
Esus
F
Fsus
F5
long - er two spac - es, where the veil that's be - tween them's so ut - ter - ly thin, that I swear I could prac - ti - cally

62
F sus
G
G sus
G5
take a peak in, where I sense in an in-stant Your pres-ence so clear-ly, to know that You love me most
66
G sus
A
A sus
D sus/A
A
tru-ly and dear-ly! Now here I stand in this Ho -
72
A sus
G/A
A
A sus
D sus/A
ly Land, stand-ing hand in hand with the

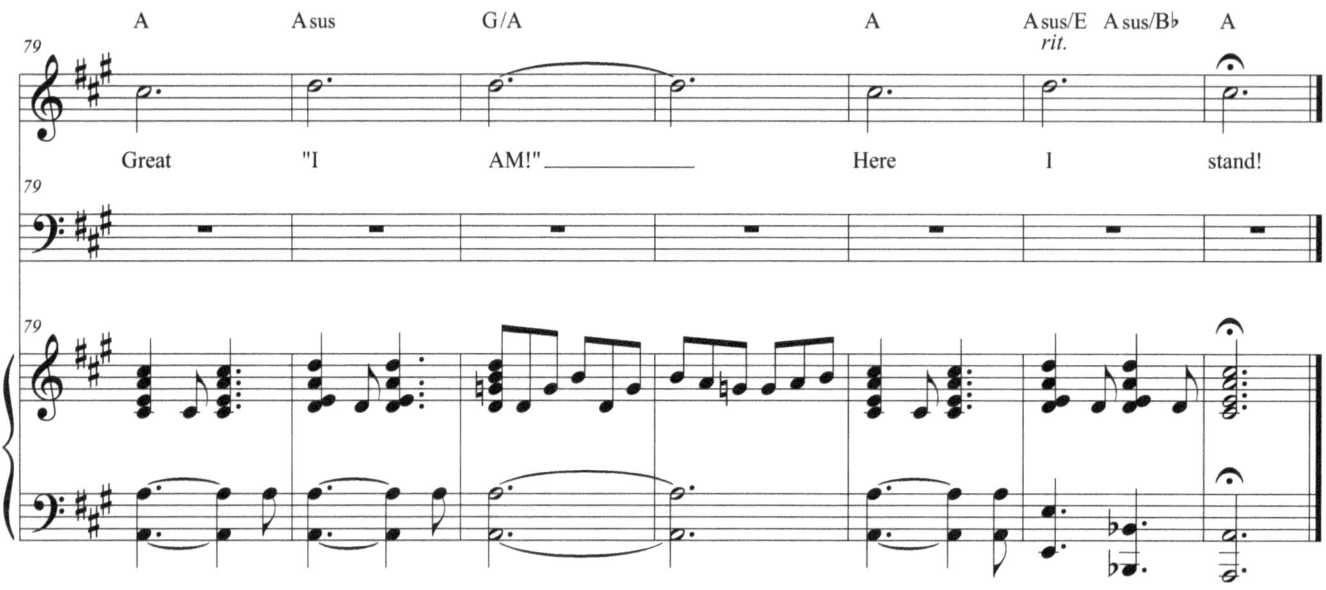
A
A sus
G/A
A
A sus/E
A sus/B♭
A
rit.
79
Great "I AM!" Here I stand!

cue:
YOUNG DIMITRI: "Over here!"
SAMMY: "Over here!"
RUTHIE: "Over here!"

7. Oranges And Lemons And Limes!

from His Name Was Nicholas

Eric Elder

♩ = 120

Voice

Piano

G sus G sus C

YOUNG DIMITRI:

I found some

4

C Csus/F

SAMMY: RUTHIE: NICHOLAS:

orang - es here! I found some lem - ons there! I found some limes right here, and I'll be glad to share! We're going to

8

G sus G sus

ALL:

take a trip, see where it all be - gan. We're going to walk, walk, walk, walk,

11

C F G Em

YOUNG DIMITRI: SAMMY:

walk three days un - til we're there! Who is this man? Why does he care? What will we do when

F F G Am B♭ B♭
RUTHIE:
we get there? I'm not sure what this day might bring. It could be al-most an-y-thing! Catch me if you
Gsus G C
YOUNG DIMITRI:
SAMMY:
RUTHIE:
dare! I found some bread right here! There's fet-a cheese right there! I found some
Csus/F Gsus
NICHOLAS:
ALL:
spic-es here. I think this price is fair! We're going to take a trip, see where it all be-gan. We're going to
Gsus C F G
YOUNG DIMITRI:
SAMMY:
run, run, run, run, run three days un-til we're there! Could this be what real faith looks like? I

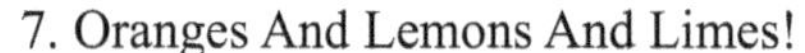

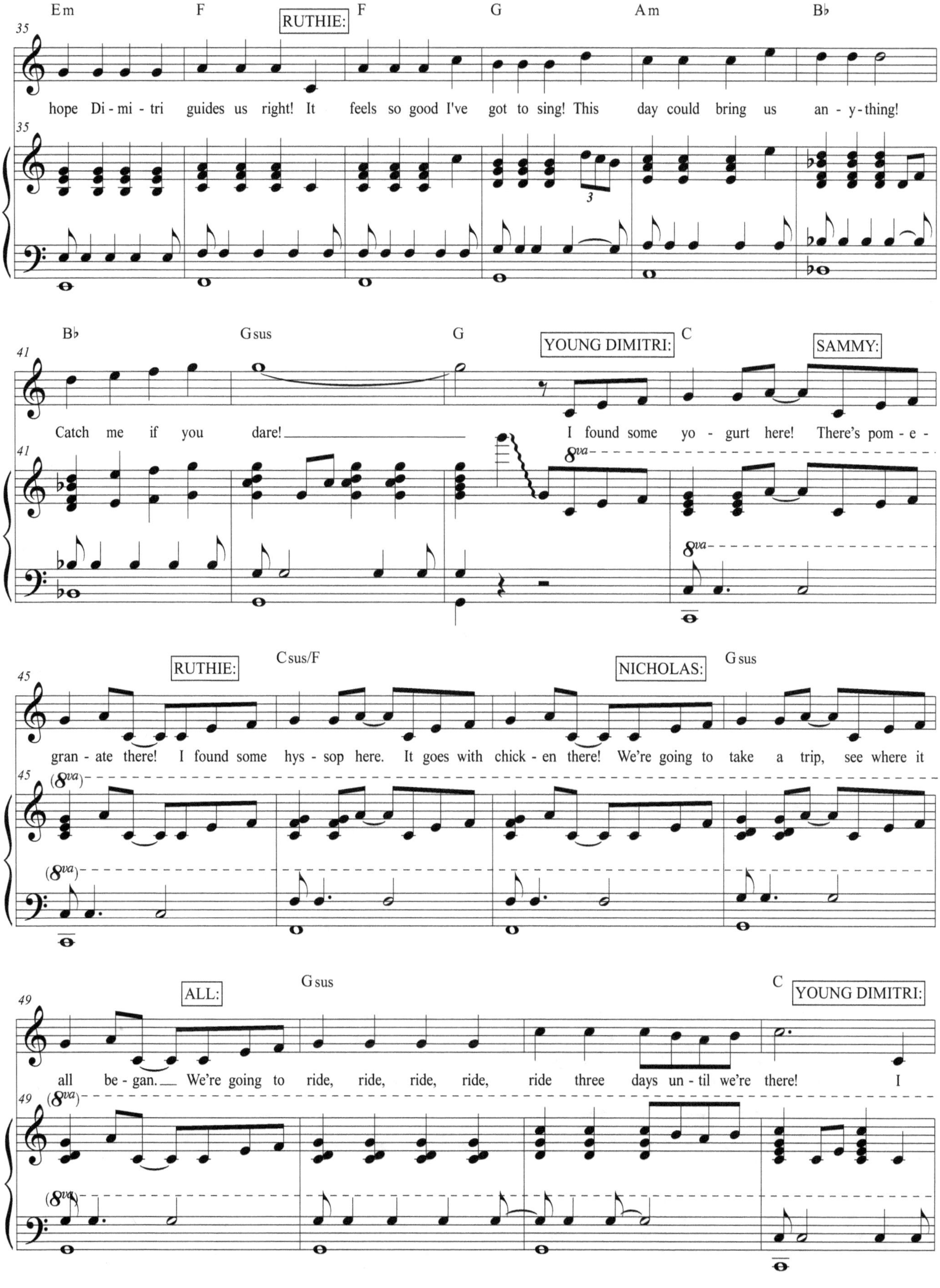
Em F RUTHIE: F G Am B♭
35
hope Di-mi-tri guides us right! It feels so good I've got to sing! This day could bring us an-y-thing!
B♭ Gsus G YOUNG DIMITRI: C SAMMY:
41
Catch me if you dare! I found some yo-gurt here! There's pom-e-
8va
RUTHIE: Csus/F NICHOLAS: Gsus
45
gran-ate there! I found some hys-sop here. It goes with chick-en there! We're going to take a trip, see where it
(8va)
ALL: Gsus C YOUNG DIMITRI:
49
all be-gan. We're going to ride, ride, ride, ride, ride three days un-til we're there! I
(8va)

F
G
SAMMY:
Em
F
RUTHIE:
F
G
won - der what we'll learn out there? I feel a change is in the air. My heart is do - ing cra - zy things! I
(8va)
Am
B♭
B♭
ALL:
Gsus
G
feel like I've been giv - en wings! Catch me if you dare!
loco
Gsus
G
Gsus
rit.
G
♩ = 96
I found some
C
accel.
Csus/F
orang - es here! I found some lem - ons there! I found some limes right here, and I'll be glad to share! We're going to

G sus
G sus
rit.
C
73
take a trip, see where it all be-gan. We're going to walk, walk, walk, walk, walk three days un-til we're there!
73

cue:
NICHOLAS:
"Everything we have comes from God anyway, doesn't it?"
8. There's Always Something You Can Give
from His Name Was Nicholas
Eric Elder
♩ = 88
Asus24/G
D
NICHOLAS:
D
Em
Voice
Piano
There's al - ways some-thing you can give. Look a -
Dmaj7
Em
A
D
Em
Dmaj7
round and you will see, wheth-er gold or gold - en flowers that live on the hills be - neath your
Em
A
D
Em
D
feet. E - ven though we know all things come from a -
Em
A
D
Em
D
Em
A
bove, still there's no great-er show of our hearts than to give in

Asus24/G
D
D
Em
Dmaj7
19
love.
There's al - ways some - thing you can give. Look in - side and you will
Em A D Em Dmaj7 Em A
24
see that your heart is where true bless - ings live. What a gift true love can be! E - ven
D Em D Em A
29
though we know all things come from a - bove, still there's
D Em D Em A Asus24/G
33
no great - er show of our hearts than to give in love.

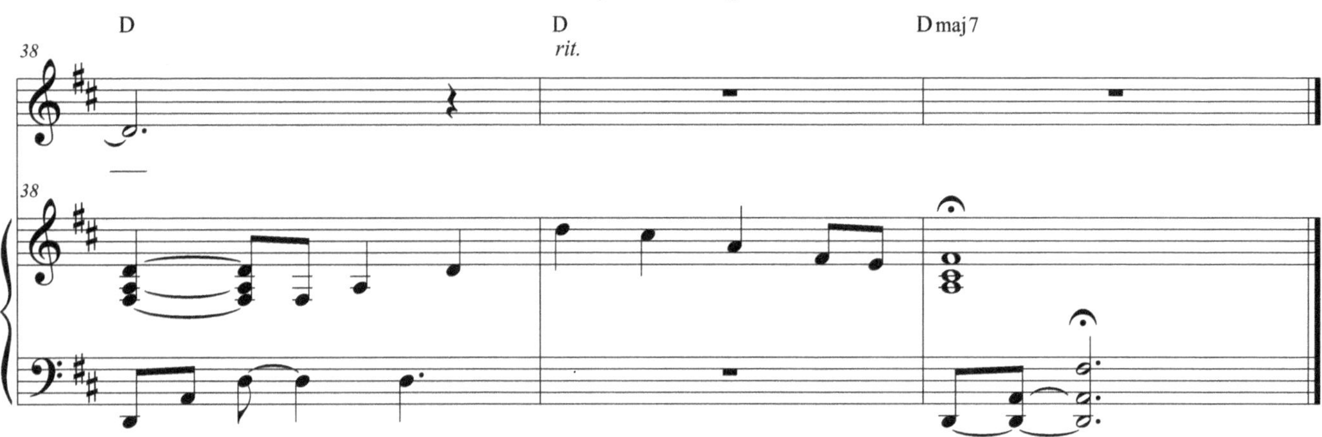
D
D
rit.
Dmaj7
38
38

cue:
NICHOLAS:
"There's always something you can give, isn't there?"
9. There's Always Something (Reprise)
from His Name Was Nicholas
Eric Elder
♩= 88
Voice
Piano
D Em D Em A
D Em D Em A Asus24/G
D E F♯m Emaj7 F♯m B
CHOIR:
There's al-ways some-thing you can give. Look a-round and you will see, wheth-er
E F♯m Emaj7 F♯m E
gold or gold-en flowers that live on the hills be-neath your feet. E-ven though we

F♯m
E
F♯m
21
know all things come from a - bove, still there's
E
F♯m
E
F♯m
24
no great-er show of our hearts than to give in
Bsus24/A
E
rit.
E
Emaj7
28
love.

cue:
SHIP'S CAPTAIN:
"So storm or no storm, you've got to go on."
NICHOLAS: "Storm or no storm, so do you."

10. Storm Or No Storm

from His Name Was Nicholas

Eric Elder

G/E
Cmaj7
B
NICHOLAS:
E
go You will guide me loud and clear. Storm or no
F♯
G
A
B
storm, the Spir - it says go, so let it blow!
E
SHIP'S CAPTAIN:
F♯
G
A
Storm or no storm, my spir - it says go, so
B
D
C
ALL
Cdim
let it blow! Oh, o - oh, o -

B
Bm
E/B
D/B
A/B
33
oh! Some-thing's stir - ring in the air to-night, I can feel it all a -
Bm
Bm
E/B
D/B
D
37
round. Some-thing's stir - ring in my soul all right, I can feel my heart - beat
F#sus
F#
G
Em
C
41
pound. And I know where - 'er I go You will go so I won't
Bsus
B
G
G/E
Cmaj7
45
fear. And I know where-'er I go You will guide me loud and

B E F♯ G A
49
clear. Storm or no storm, the Spir - it says go, so
B E F♯ G
54
let it blow! Storm or no storm, my spir - it says
A B D C
58
go, so let it blow! Oh, o -
C Am/C C7 B
62
rit.
oh, o - - - oh!

cue:
NICHOLAS:
"Even if it feels like we're in the center of a hurricane."

11. He's The Song

from His Name Was Nicholas

Eric Elder

that would hold me back, to take
Csus24/F
hold of Him who knows no
Fsus
C(add2)
C
F2
lack.
Stay the course, hold on
Gsus
G
C
F2
Gsus
G
tight, let the dark be cast out by His light. He's the

F
C/E
Dm7
Gsus
G
F
23
calm, He's the calm, He's the calm in the rag-ing of the sea. He's the calm, He's the
C/E
Dm7
Gsus
C
28
calm, He's the calm who com - forts me. I could
C(add2)
32
write a song of His love for
28
Csus24/F
34
me, how He lived and died,

C(add2)

36
— gave His life for — me. But I've

Gsus(add6)

38
heard that He — wrote a song for

F2

40
me, and the song He sings —

C2

42
— is both wild and — free.

C F2 Gsus G C
44
Stay the course, don't you pout, let His
44
F2 Gsus G F C/E
49
song drive the dark - ness out. He's the song, He's the song, He's the
49
Dm7 Gsus G F C/E
54
song in the danc - ing of the sea. He's the song, He's the song, He's the
54
Dm7 Gsus C F C/E
58
song who com-pos - es me. He's the song, He's the song, He's the
58

Dm7
Gsus
G
F
C/E
62
song in the danc - ing of the sea. He's the song, He's the song, He's the
Dm7
Gsus
F
C/E
Dm7
C
rit.
66
song who com-pos - es me.

cue:
NICHOLAS:
"And because of the storm, we might actually make it there on time."

12. Storm Or No Storm (Reprise)

from His Name Was Nicholas

Eric Elder

♩ = 94

CREW MATES:

Voice

Piano

B E F♯ G

Storm or no storm, the Spir - it says

5

A B E F♯

go, so let it blow! Storm or no storm, my

9

G A B D

spir - it says go, so let it blow!

A

13

C C Am/C C7 B

rit.

Oh, o - oh, O - oh.

cue:
NICHOLAS:
"Round up the crew!
I'll speak to the people.
I know just where we'll go."

13. He's The Song (Reprise)

from His Name Was Nicholas

Eric Elder

14. His Name Was Nicholas

from His Name Was Nicholas

Eric Elder

PRIEST #3:
D
PRIEST #1:
A sus
PRIEST #3:
D
PRIEST #2:
A sus
PRIEST #3:
That's what I said! His name was Ni-cho-las. May-be Ic-a-rus? Clear-ly Ni-cho-las. Now don't tick-le us! No, I'm
D G D/F♯ Em D
PRIEST #2:
A sus
PRIEST #3:
se-ri-ous! And he's quite a man. His name was Ni-cho-las. Don't be friv-o-lous! I'm me-
D
PRIEST #1:
A sus
PRIEST #3:
D G D/F♯ Em D Em7
tic-u-lous. Dreams can crip-ple us. Dreams de-liv-er us as they of-ten have. Re-mem-ber Jo-seph in his cell? Two
D/F♯ G2
PRIEST #1:
D Em7
PRIEST #2:
D/F♯ G2
PRIEST #1:
dreams to him, two men did tell. Both dreams came true in three days time, and Jo-seph was freed from his crime. And the

Asus
A
Asus
A
PRIEST #2:
Asus
Asus
27
oth - er Jo - seph, just as true, he had a dream one night like you. The name of Je - sus came to him straight
27
Asus
A
D/F♯
A/E
A
PRIEST #3:
30
from an an - gel, not a whi - m. And you be - lieve him?!? His name was
30
D
PRIEST #1:
Asus
PRIEST #3:
D
PRIEST #2:
Asus
PRIEST #3:
D
G
D/F♯
34
Ni - cho - las. And he'll vis - it us? He will vis - it us. Doubt the lit - tlest? God will give to us some - one from His
34
Em
D
PRIEST #1:
Asus
PRIEST #3:
D
PRIEST #2:
Asus
PRIEST #3:
37
hand. His name was Ni - cho - las. It's fe - lic - i - tous! It's just Ni - cho - las. And he'll vis - it us? He will
37

40
D G D/F♯ Em PRIEST #1: D Em7 D/F♯ G2 PRIEST #2:
vis-it us right here where we stand. Per-haps we'll ask God for a sign to make it clear what's on His mind. We'll
44
D Em7 D/F♯ G2 PRIEST #1: A sus A
ask Him to bring through that door the bish-op we've been look-ing for. The one that God will give to us will
47
A sus A PRIEST #2: A sus A sus A sus A D/F♯ A/E
have the name of Ni-cho-las. That would be un-de-ni-a-ble and prove dreams are re-li - a - b -
51
A PRIEST #3: D Esus A7 D
PRIEST #1: PRIEST #2: PRIEST #3:
le. Don't hold me li-a-ble! But... His name was Ni-cho-las! Ni-cho-las!!! Ni-cho-las!!! Ni-cho-las!!!

cue:
PRIEST #3: "God always gives us a choice, Nicholas. The Holy Spirit, He is... a gentleman."

15. This Day At The Crossroads

from His Name Was Nicholas

Eric Elder

Eb/Ab
Eb/Bb
Bb
PRIEST #3:
Eb
PRIEST #1:
Ab6/9
PRIEST #3:
17
lead not just one church, but more in this land? His name was Ni-cho-las! I am so im-pressed! It was
Eb
PRIEST #2:
Ab6/9
PRIEST #3:
Eb
Ab Eb/G Fm
20
Ni-cho-las. We are heav-en blessed! He walked through that door, and I al-most cried. His name was
Eb
PRIEST #1:
Ab6/9
PRIEST #3:
Eb
PRIEST #2:
Ab9
PRIEST #3:
Eb
Ab Eb/G
23
Ni-cho-las! We will be just fine. It was Ni-cho-las. We just need some time. But now Ni-cho-las, what will he de-
Fm
NICHOLAS:
Eb
Ab/F
Eb/G
Ab
Eb
Ab/F
26
cide? But can I make the sac-ri-fice? A lov-ing wife, a fam-i-ly? What if the life I've dreamed a-bout is

Eb/G Ab Bbsus Bb Bbsus Bb
diff-'rent from Your dreams for me? I want to want what You want, Lord! I know that You have dreams ga-lore! Please
Bbsus Bbsus Bbsus Bb Eb/G Bb/F Bb Bbsus
help me, Lord, to un-der-stand. Please help me, Lord, I'm just a ma - n.
Ebmaj7
There is a way that seems right to a man. In the
Cm7 Ab/C Cm7 Ab/C Ab Eb/Ab Ab Eb/Ab
end, all that mat-ters is what's in Your plan. What we give up on earth up in heav - en is found, the

Eb/Ab
Eb/Bb
Bb
Ebmaj7
47
blessing of family and love all around. My answer is "Yes, Lord," no matter the question. To
Cm7
Ab/C
Cm7
Ab/C
Ab
Eb/Ab
Ab
Eb/Ab
51
You I pour out all my love and affection. Seal this on my lips, help me never to waver. This
Eb/Ab
Eb/Bb
Bb
PRIESTS:
Eb
CREW MATES:
PRIESTS:
55
day at the crossroads I'll forever savor. His name was Nicholas! Here's to Nicholas! It was
Eb
CREW MATES:
PRIESTS:
Eb
Ab
Eb/G
Fm
ALL:
59
Nicholas! Cheers for Nicholas! God has given us someone from His hand. His name was

Eb
Ab6/9
Eb
Ab6/9
NICHOLAS:
Ni-cho-las! Here's to Ni-cho-las! It was Ni-cho-las! Cheers for Ni-cho-las! Thanks, but
Ab Eb/G Fm
ALL:
Eb
Fsus
Bb7
Eb
real-ly! I am just a man! His name was Ni-cho-las! Ni-cho-las!!! Ni-cho-las!!! Ni-cho-las!!!

cue:
CASSIUS: "And I can't let you go without saying it again... and again... and again..."
16. Sophia!
from His Name Was Nicholas
Eric Elder
Voice
Piano
CASSIUS:
So - phi-a, I love you with my whole heart!
So - phi-a, I love you with my soul!
So - phi-a, I love you with an ev - er-last - ing love!
So - phi-a, you're the half who makes me whole!
I love you more than you'll be - lieve! I love you

F G F C
more than you can pos-sib-ly re-ceive! But still I'll try to tell you why, 'cause I'll keep
F G A♭ D♭
lov-ing you long past the day I die, and here's why! So-phi-a, I
G♭ D♭ G♭ A♭sus A♭ D♭ G♭
love you with my whole heart! So-phi-a, I love you with my
A♭sus A♭ G♭/B♭ A♭/C B♭m E♭m D♭/F
soul! So-phi-a, I love you with an ev-er-last-ing

G♭ B♭m A♭ G♭ D♭
love! So - phi - a, you're the half who makes me whole! I could
G♭ D♭ G♭ A♭
look at you for hours and not get bored! Day af - ter day I love you more! I can't
G♭ D♭ G♭ A♭
think of you with - out a bit of blush - ing, 'cause the blood in my heart, it just starts gush - ing!
A♭ A♭ D♭ G♭ D♭
rit.
a tempo
So - phi - a, I love you with my whole heart!
15ma
8va

G♭ A♭sus A♭ D♭ G♭ A♭sus
So - phi - a, I love you with my soul!
A♭ G♭/B♭ A♭/C B♭m E♭ D♭/F
So - phi - a, I love you with an ev - er - last - ing
G♭ B♭m A♭ G♭ D♭/F
rit.
love! So - phi - a, you're the half who makes me whole!
E♭m7 D♭
The half who makes me whole!

cue:
SOPHIA: "You know I wouldn't do it if it was anyone else asking me."
YOUNG ANNA MARIA: "I know."
17. Sophia! (Reprise)
from His Name Was Nicholas
Eric Elder
♩=92
SOPHIA:
Voice
Piano
G♭ D♭ G♭ D♭
I love you more than you'll be - lieve. I love you
G♭ A♭ G♭ D♭
more than you can pos-sib-ly re - ceive. But still I'll try to tell you why, 'cause I'll keep
G♭ A♭
lo-ving you long past the day I die...
MIGEL: ... it had to be God who answered our prayers.
A♭ G♭ D♭/F
E♭m7 D♭

cue:
NICHOLAS: "I'd love to hear it."
YOUNG ANNA MARIA: "I could sing it now?"

18. Like A Mirror To My Heart!

from His Name Was Nicholas

Eric Elder

♩ = 92

Voice

Piano

Am F F7/D C/G C C

YOUNG ANNA MARIA:

I be - lieve there is

F2 C F2 C F2

6 some - one just for me, there must be some - one, though I can't see, I know that some - day I'll find

Gsus G C F2 C

11 love. I be - lieve there is some - one just for me, there must be

F2 C F2 Gsus G

16 some - one, my des - ti - ny, sent down from heav - en a - bove. And I

Am G F C/E
21
know ___ there's some - one for __ me, e - ven if ___ we're miles a - part, ___ re - flect - ing
Dm C F G C
25
who ___ I'm meant to be, ___ like a mir - ror to my heart. ___ Oh, I be - lieve, ___ Oh, I be -
Am F F/G G C Am
30
lieve, ___ Oh, I be - lieve there is some - one. Oh, I be - lieve, ___ Oh, I be - lieve, ___ Oh, I be -
F F/G G F C/E Dm7
35
lieve there is some - one just for me, just for me, just for me, just for

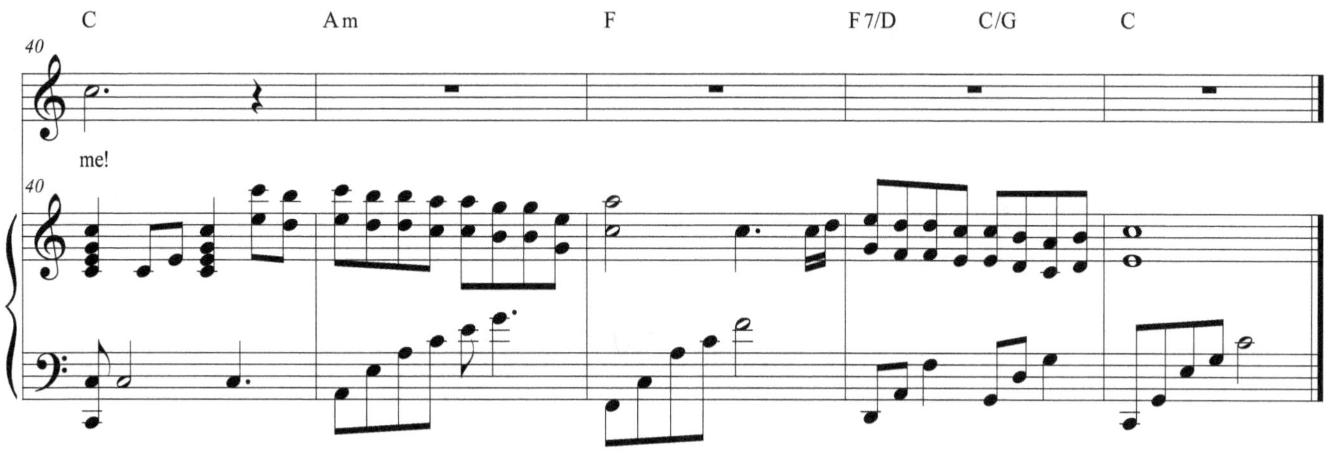
C
Am
F
F7/D
C/G
C
40
me!
40

cue:
CECILIA:
"Nicholas, you say?"

19. Like A Mirror To My Heart (Reprise)

from His Name Was Nicholas

Eric Elder

cue:
NICHOLAS: "I just need to know... You're still with me."

20. My Sanctuary

from His Name Was Nicholas

Eric Elder

B♭m F/A Gm F B♭/F C/F

pres - ence. Oh, Lord, bring me there! Bring me home. Into Your

F B♭6 F B♭6 Dm7

sanc-tu-ar-y, Oh, Lord! In-to the place that You call Your home. In-to Your sanc-tu-ar-y, Oh,

C/E F B♭ Csus C

Lord! For I know when I'm there I'm not a - lone! All I

F Dm B♭maj7 C F

want, all I need, is to be with You and to know You're near. All I want, all I

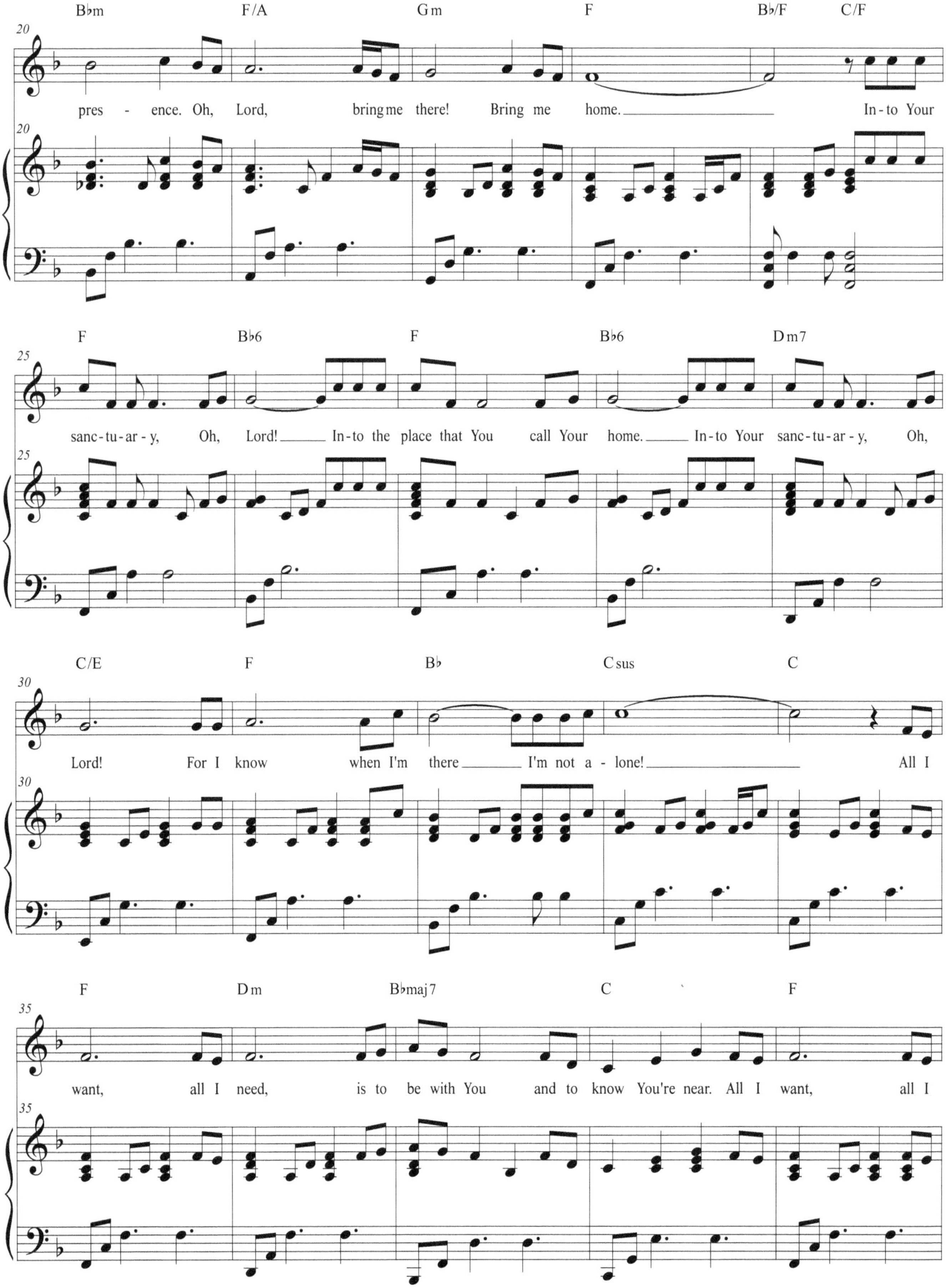

Dm Bbmaj7 C F Am
need, is to talk with You and to know You'll hear. And I know there's a place I can
Bb Bbm F/A Gm F
go to feel Your pres - ence. Oh, Lord, bring me there! Bring me home.
Bb/F C/F F Bb6 F Bb6
This is my sanc-tu-ar-y, Oh, Lord! This is the place that I call my home. This is my
Dm7 C/E F Bb Csus
sanc-tu-ar-y, Oh, Lord! For I know when I'm here I'm not a - lone!

C
Dsus
D
G
Em
I'm not a - lone!
All I want, all I need, is to
C
G/D
D
G
Em
C
be in Your pres - ence. All I want, all I need, is to be in Your
G/D
D
G
Em7
C2
VOICE OF GOD:
This is my sanc-tu-ar-y. This is my sanc-tu-ar-y. This is my sanc-tu-ar-y. This is my
pres - ence. All I want, all I need, is to be in Your

G/D D G Em7 C2
ho - me! This is my sanc-tu-ar-y. This is my sanc-tu-ar-y. This is my sanc-tu-ar-y. This is my
pres - ence. All I want, all I need, is to be in Your
G/D rit. D G Gm/B♭
ho - me!
pres - ence. This is my sanc-tu-ar-y. This is my sanc-tu-ar-y. This is my
C2 rit. G
sanc - tu - ar - y. This is my home!

cue:
DIMITRI: "I will. But I can't just tell it! I have to sing it!"

21. Catch Me! I'm Falling In Love!

from His Name Was Nicholas

Eric Elder

DIMITRI:

In my jour-ney to find where you might be, I met on my way... An-na Ma-ri-a. "Have a flow-er?" she said, and I nod-ded my head, then I found words and said, "So nice to meet ya!" "Is there some-one named Ni-cho-las a-round?" And she gasped and dropped to the ground! Then a sto-ry she told a-bout two bags of gold. I grew sud-den-ly bold for a

Dm7/A Ab dim7 Gm7 Bb/C Dm/F Bbmaj7/C Am7/C Gm7/C Am7/C Gm7
third bag to hold as my heart had be-gun to un-fold.
Gm7 Gsus7/C C(add2) Bbmaj7 C/Bb Am7 Abdim7 Gm7 C
To her win-dow I ran, with the gold in my hand I had earned in that most Ho-ly
C(add6)/F Eb/C F7 Bbmaj7 C/Bb Am7 Abdim7 Gm7 C
Land. Set the bag down in-side, then I ran off to hide, pray-ing some-day we'd sit side by
C(add6)/F G/E A7(9) D6/9 Gm7 Bb6/E A13 A7(#5)
side. Then I prayed that some-how I'd find you. God grant-ed that prayer num-ber two!

D7(9) D7(♭9) B♭maj7 C/B♭ Am7 A♭dim7 Gm7 A♭dim7
37
Back to prayer num - ber one, not to say you're not fun, but sweet An - na Ma - ri - a, she's
Dm7/A A♭dim7 Gm7 B♭/C Cm/A Csus(b2)/E♭ D7 Gm7 B♭dim/C
41
nat - u - ral - ly a bright an - gel from heav - en a - bove! Catch me! I'm fal - ling in
B♭maj7/C Am7/C Gm7/C Am7/C Gm7 B♭/C F2
45
lo - - - - ve! La - dee - da, la - dee - da - da!

cue:
NICHOLAS and DIMITRI take their seats, then a CHILDREN'S CHOIR enters and begins to sing.

22. Wisps Of Smoke

from His Name Was Nicholas

Eric Elder

NICHOLAS:
F(add2) B♭ A♭/C B♭/D E♭ F(add2)
new. I nev-er thought I'd see what lies be - fore me in plain view. I won-der,
B♭ A♭/C B♭/D E♭ F(add2)
"Could it be a breath of life as I once knew?"
CHILDREN'S CHOIR & NICHOLAS:
Cm7 B♭
A new time, A new sea - son, A
Cm7 B♭ A♭(add2)
new start, A new rea - son, A new dawn, A new

22. Wisps Of Smoke

Cm7
Dm
E♭
F(add2)
B♭
Cm7
Gm/D
B♭sus/E♭
F(add2)
45
of - fering un - to You. Ris - ing up, cre - at - ing some - thing fresh and new.
45

cue:
MASTER OF CEREMONIES:
"Next we hear from Arius of Alexandria... speaking on the divinity."

23. Just A Man

from His Name Was Nicholas

Eric Elder

F/C C Dm/C C
ARIUS:
C C C Fm/A♭ C/G
18
this done! They are all div-i-ni-ty.
He was cer-tain-ly spe-cial, I'll grant you that. But
C C C B♭ C C Fm/A♭ C/G
23
noth-ing like God. He was just a man. Just a man, I say, like you and like me, per-haps a
C B♭ C C C F/C F/C C C Dm/C
NICHOLAS:
27
few bars short of div-i-ni-ty. Just a man, you say? Just a man, you say? Just like you and like me?
C C F/C F/C C Dm/C C
32
Please don't kid with me. You're just kid-ding me. He's a De-i-ty!

C C C Fm/A♭ C/G C C
ARIUS:
He did great things, but by his Fa-ther's hand, not by an-y-thing he had planned.
C B♭ C C C C A♭ C/G C C
He was just a man, I say. Just a good, sec-ond best. To say an-y-thing else
C B♭ C C C F/C F/C
NICHOLAS:
would make God some-how less. Sec - ond best, you say? Some - how less, you say?
C C Dm/C C C F/C F/C
God, who would ev-er have guessed? My fa-ther and moth-er both lived and died for Him.

C Dm/C C C F/C G/C C C F/C
I am not im - pressed.
I am a-live be-cause Je-sus died! I am a-live be-cause
G/C C C F/C G/C C C F/C G/C C
Je-sus died! I am a-live be-cause Je-sus died! I am a-live be-cause Je-sus died!
C C C A♭ C/G C C
ARIUS:
Look who's talking, it's Ni-cho-las, right? I heard you were like-ly to
C B♭ C C C C A♭ C/G C C
put up a fight. Well, put 'em up now, come on and jump in the ring, I'll duke it out with an-y-one, and

C Bb C C C F/C F/C C C Dm7/C
70
NICHOLAS:
I ev-en sing. With Con-stan-tine here, it is pro - per and fit-ting that we all stay si-lent and just
Dm7/C C C F/C F/C C Dm7/C C
74
keep on sit-ting. But how can we sit here and not say a word when his words stream out, de-mean-
C C F/C G/C C C F/C
78
ing our Lord? I did-n't spend those ten years in a jail to lis-ten to this man tell his
G/C C C F/C G/C C C F/C
82
pleas-ant tale. I've been beat-en, I've been tor-tured, just like the rest, for our One True Mes-si-ah, our

G/C C
ARIUS:
C C C B♭/C
God in the flesh. But what will the bish-ops e-ven-tually con-clude?
C C C B♭sus4/C C C C B♭/C
That's all that mat-ters and not what he's brewed. What if the flock in the cen-turies a-head starts
C C C B♭sus4/C C C F/C F/C
NICHOLAS:
fol-low-ing my words and think-ing in-stead? He is love, He is life, and what I love the most, He
C C Dm/C Dm/C C C F/C F/C C Dm/C
lives in me through the Ho - ly Ghost. He is tru-ly the Liv - ing Vine, ful-ly hu-man and

C
C C C F/C G/C C C F/C
ful - ly di - vine. Like those who killed Je - sus the first time a - round, you're do - ing it a - gain, right
G/C C C F/C G/C C C F/C
here and right now. In their zeal to de - fend God, they had it all back - wards. They killed Him in - stead, those in -
G/C C C C Fm/A♭ C/G C C
MASTER OF CEREMONIES:
ARIUS:
cre - di - ble... Men, in - door voic - es. Show us your proof, your ev - i - dence, sir, of his e - ter - nal pres - ence, his
C B♭ C C C C Fm/A♭ C/G C C C B♭ C
NICHOLAS:
di - vine na - ture. What makes you think that you're smart - er than me? Show us your proof and then let it be. It was

B♭ F/A Gsus E♭ D♭ C B♭ F/A
118
not on a whim on a cross He was hung, but for say-ing that "I and the Fa-ther are one." "I'm in my Fa-ther, and
Gsus E♭ D♭ C Cm Fm/C B♭/C Cm
123
He is in Me." That's what He said be-fore dy-ing for me. They put Him to death for speak-ing the truth.
Cm Fm/C Dm6/C Cm Cm A♭/C B♭/C Cm
128
Yet, here you stand, ask-ing for more proof? Well, my ev-i-dence is here, right where I stand.
Cm A♭/C Dm6/C Cm C C C Fm/A♭ C/G C C C B♭ C
132
I did-n't get these for "just a man."

ARIUS:
139
Well, then it looks, sir, like you were mis - tak - en. As I was say - ing...
Cm Fm/C Dm6/C Cm
143
Cm Fm/C Dm6/C Cm Cm Ab/C Bb/C Cm Cm Ab/C
148
Dm6/C Cm Cm Ab/C Bb/C Cm Cm Ab/C Dm6/C Cm
153
Cm Ab/C Bb/C Cm Cm Ab/C Dm6/C Cm
(punch)

cue:
NICHOLAS: "Dimitri, God has set me free again... in more ways than one."

24. Healing Comes From Heaven (Reprise)

from His Name Was Nicholas

Eric Elder

D♭/B♭
E♭
E♭
F
B♭
E♭
13
hard-ly un-der-stand. Some-times it takes so long, but then we stand! And we can al-ways know that
D♭/B♭
D♭/A♭
D♭sus/G♭
B♭
rit.
17
one day we will be made whole when heav-en comes to stay.

25. St. Nick's Theme/His Name Was Nicholas (Reprise)

cue:
DIMITRI: "But if we live it right, as Nicholas did, one life is all we need."

from His Name Was Nicholas

Eric Elder

25. St. Nick's Theme/His Name Was Nicholas (Reprise)

43
E♭
A♭6/9
E♭
A♭6/9
46
E♭
A♭
E♭/G
F m
E♭
A♭6/9
49
E♭
A♭9
E♭
A♭
E♭/G
F m
52
E♭
A♭/F
E♭/G
A♭
E♭
A♭/F
55
E♭/G
A♭
B♭sus
B♭
B♭sus
B♭
58
B♭sus
B♭sus
B♭sus
B♭
E♭/G
B♭/F
B♭
B♭sus

ALL:
E♭
A♭6/9
His name was Ni-cho-las! Here's to Ni-co-las! It was
E♭
A♭6/9
E♭
A♭
E♭/G
Fm
Ni-cho-las! Cheers for Ni-cho-las! God has giv en us some-one from His hand. His name was
E♭
A♭6/9
E♭
A♭6/9
NICHOLAS:
A♭
E♭/G
Ni-cho-las! Here's to Ni-cho-las! It was Ni-cho-las! Cheers for Ni-cho-las! Thanks, but real-ly! I am just a
F
ALL:
E♭
F sus
B♭
E♭
man! His name was Ni-cho-las! Ni-cho-las!!! Ni-cho-las!!! Ni-cho-las!!!

www.ingramcontent.com/pod-product-compliance
Lightning Source LLC
LaVergne TN
LVHW061329060426
835513LV00015B/1336

* 9 7 8 1 9 3 1 7 6 0 7 8 2 *